Getting Started with Citrix® Provisioning Services 7.0

An example-packed guide to help you successfully administer Citrix® Provisioning Services

Puthiyavan Udayakumar

[PACKT] enterprise 🟦
PUBLISHING   professional expertise distilled

BIRMINGHAM - MUMBAI

Getting Started with Citrix® Provisioning Services 7.0

First published: January 2014

Production Reference: 1200114

Published by Packt Publishing Ltd.
Livery Place
35 Livery Street
Birmingham B3 2PB, UK.

ISBN 978-1-78217-670-1

www.packtpub.com

Cover Image by Jarek Blaminsky (milak6@wp.pl)

Credits

Author
Puthiyavan Udayakumar

Reviewers
Jack Cobben

Vikash Kumar Roy

Acquisition Editors
Rubal Kaur

Mary Jasmine Nadar

Commissioning Editor
Priyanka S

Technical Editors
Kapil Hemnani

Siddhi Rane

Faisal Siddiqui

Copy Editors
Sarang Chari

Brandt D'Mello

Adithi Shetty

Project Coordinator
Ankita Goenka

Proofreader
Mario Cecere

Indexer
Rekha Nair

Graphics
Yuvraj Mannari

Production Coordinator
Arvindkumar Gupta

Cover Work
Arvindkumar Gupta

Notice

The statements made and opinions expressed herein belong exclusively to the author and reviewers of this publication, and are not shared by or represent the viewpoint of Citrix Systems®, Inc. This publication does not constitute an endorsement of any product, service, or point of view. Citrix® makes no representations, warranties or assurances of any kind, express or implied, as to the completeness, accuracy, reliability, suitability, availability, or currency of the content contained in this publication or any material related to this publication. Any reliance you place on such content is strictly at your own risk. In no event shall Citrix®, its agents, officers, employees, licensees, or affiliates be liable for any damages whatsoever (including, without limitation, damages for loss of profits, business information, or loss of information) arising out of the information or statements contained in the publication, even if Citrix® has been advised of the possibility of such loss or damages.

Citrix®, Citrix Systems®, XenApp®, XenDesktop®, and CloudPortal™ are trademarks of Citrix Systems®, Inc. and/or one or more of its subsidiaries, and may be registered in the United States Patent and Trademark Office and in other countries.

About the Author

Puthiyavan Udayakumar has more than six years of IT experience with expertise in Citrix, VMware, Microsoft products, and Apache CloudStack. He has extensive experience in designing and implementing virtualization solutions using various Citrix products, VMware Products, and Microsoft products. He is an IBM certified Solution Architect and Citrix certified Enterprise Engineer along with more than 15 certifications in infrastructure products. He is the author of the book, *Getting Started with Citrix® CloudPortal™*. He holds a master's degree in Science with a specialization in System Software from Birla Institute of Technology and Science, Pilani, a bachelor's degree in Engineering through SKR Engineering College from Anna University, and National award from the Indian Society for Technical Education. He presented various research papers in more than 15 national and international conferences including IADIS (held in Dublin, Ireland) followed by the IEEE pattern.

I would like to dedicate this book to my beloved mom, Dr.K. Mangayarkarasi, dad, Dr.P.Udayakumar, brother, Mr.Kathiravan, and to his family.

Big thanks to Packt Publishing to get this book published!

About the Reviewers

Jack Cobben, with over thirteen years of systems management experience, is no stranger to the challenges that enterprises can experience when managing large deployments of Windows systems and Citrix implementations. He writes in his free time for his own blog www.jackcobben.nl and is active on the Citrix support forums. He loves to test new software and share the knowledge in any way he can. You can follow him on twitter via @jackcobben.

Vikash Kumar Roy has been associated with associated with IT for close to 15 years. In his 15-year IT career, he worked on various platforms and domains. Currently, he is an expert on end-user computing. Prior to this, he designed and delivered solutions on server virtualization.

> I would like to thank my guru and my boss who helped me learn and deal with every challenge I faced with my current and previous job.

www.PacktPub.com

Support files, eBooks, discount offers, and more

You might want to visit www.PacktPub.com for support files and downloads related to your book.

Did you know that Packt offers eBook versions of every book published, with PDF and ePub files available? You can upgrade to the eBook version at www.PacktPub.com and as a print book customer, you are entitled to a discount on the eBook copy. Get in touch with us at service@packtpub.com for more details.

At www.PacktPub.com, you can also read a collection of free technical articles, sign up for a range of free newsletters and receive exclusive discounts and offers on Packt books and eBooks.

http://PacktLib.PacktPub.com

Do you need instant solutions to your IT questions? PacktLib is Packt's online digital book library. Here, you can access, read, and search across Packt's entire library of books.

Why Subscribe?

- Fully searchable across every book published by Packt
- Copy and paste, print, and bookmark content
- On demand and accessible via web browser

Free Access for Packt account holders

If you have an account with Packt at www.PacktPub.com, you can use this to access PacktLib today and view nine entirely free books. Simply use your login credentials for immediate access.

Instant Updates on New Packt Books

Get notified! Find out when new books are published by following @PacktEnterprise on Twitter, or the *Packt Enterprise* Facebook page.

Table of Contents

Preface

Citrix® Provisioning Services fulfills the need of virtual disk streaming over networks. The product allows virtual disks to be provisioned and reprovisioned in real time from a single shared disk image or from a dedicated disk. The product also aids to avoid the necessity to manage and patch discrete systems. Instead, all image management is through the master image, and this results in a reduction of power usage, system failure rates, and security risks.

Citrix® Provisioning Services shrinks the total cost of ownership and improves both manageability and business agility, along with the cost over operational expenditure. The attractiveness of this particular product is that a single read-only image can be concurrently streamed to compound diskless targets, both physical and virtual.

Getting Started with Citrix® Provisioning Services 7.0 will accompany a Citrix® Provisioning Services administrator looking to understand Citrix® Provisioning features, architecture, terminology used, installation and configuration, operating and managing farm, store, sites, views, and Citrix® Provisioning Server.

With *Getting Started with Citrix® Provisioning Services 7.0*, you will learn about the concepts and administration of the Citrix® Provisioning Server.

What this book covers

Chapter 1, Introduction to Citrix® Provisioning Services 7.0, explains how to get started with Citrix® Provisioning Services, product overview, essentials of products, features fulfilling the real-world needs, the logical flow and technical architecture of the product, and the terminology and system requirement to install provisioning services.

Chapter 2, Installing and Configuring Citrix® Provisioning Services 7.0, covers installation and configuration of Citrix® Provisioning Services, Citrix® Provisioning Services Console using graphical user interface and using a command-line interface.

Chapter 3, Managing Citrix® Provisioning Disk, explains about organizing a (master) principal target device aimed at imaging, constructing a vDisk image, creating a vDisk, allocating vDisk to the target disk, followed by dealing with bootstrap files and booting devices.

Chapter 4, Operating Citrix® Provisioning Services 7.0, covers managing and operating farms, sites, stores, target devices, target device collection, Provisioning Server, view, and creating a vDisk.

Chapter 5, Upgrading Citrix® Provisioning Farm and vDisk, explains about requirements, mandate action to upgrade Citrix® Provisioning Services, upgrading vDisk, and a list reference article that helps in basic troubleshooting for administrators/engineers.

What you need for this book

Required operating system is Windows Server 2012. We can download it from `http://technet.microsoft.com/en-in/evalcenter/hh670538.aspx`.

Required Citrix source is Citrix Provisioning Service 7.x. We can download it from `http://www.citrix.com/downloads.html`.

Who this book is for

This book helps people who are actively looking for jobs in the IT industry, as well as people working in the IT industry, those who want to skill themselves towards Citrix® CloudPortal™, along with the following various roles where this book will be essential:

- Citrix® XenApp® Virtualization Administrator, Engineer, Architect.
- Citrix® XenDesktop® Administrator, Engineer, Architect.
- Citrix® Provisioning Services Administrator, Engineer, Architect.
- Physical/Blade Server Administrator, Engineer, Architect.
- Virtualization administrator

Conventions

In this book, you will find a number of styles of text that distinguish between different kinds of information. Here are some examples of these styles and an explanation of their meaning.

Code words in text, database table names, folder names, filenames, file extensions, pathnames, dummy URLs, user input, and Twitter handles are shown as follows: "Run `ConfigWizard.exe` with the `/?` parameter."

Any command-line input or output is written as follows:

```
<Installer Name>.exe /s /v"/qn"
```

New terms and **important words** are shown in bold. Words that you see on the screen, in menus or dialog boxes for example, appear in the text like this: "On your screen, the **Provisioning Services** wizard appears. Click on **Server Installation**."

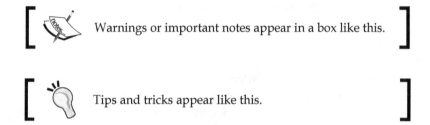

> Warnings or important notes appear in a box like this.

> Tips and tricks appear like this.

Reader feedback

Feedback from our readers is always welcome. Let us know what you think about this book—what you liked or may have disliked. Reader feedback is important for us to develop titles that you really get the most out of.

To send us general feedback, simply send an e-mail to `feedback@packtpub.com`, and mention the book title via the subject of your message.

If there is a topic that you have expertise in and you are interested in either writing or contributing to a book, see our author guide on `www.packtpub.com/authors`.

Customer support

Now that you are the proud owner of a Packt book, we have a number of things to help you to get the most from your purchase.

Errata

Although we have taken every care to ensure the accuracy of our content, mistakes do happen. If you find a mistake in one of our books—maybe a mistake in the text or the code—we would be grateful if you would report this to us. By doing so, you can save other readers from frustration and help us improve subsequent versions of this book. If you find any errata, please report them by visiting http://www.packtpub.com/submit-errata, selecting your book, clicking on the **errata submission form** link, and entering the details of your errata. Once your errata are verified, your submission will be accepted and the errata will be uploaded on our website, or added to any list of existing errata, under the Errata section of that title. Any existing errata can be viewed by selecting your title from http://www.packtpub.com/support.

Piracy

Piracy of copyright material on the Internet is an ongoing problem across all media. At Packt, we take the protection of our copyright and licenses very seriously. If you come across any illegal copies of our works, in any form, on the Internet, please provide us with the location address or website name immediately so that we can pursue a remedy.

Please contact us at copyright@packtpub.com with a link to the suspected pirated material.

We appreciate your help in protecting our authors, and our ability to bring you valuable content.

Questions

You can contact us at questions@packtpub.com if you are having a problem with any aspect of the book, and we will do our best to address it.

1
Introduction to Citrix® Provisioning Services 7.0

Thank you for picking up *Getting Started with Citrix® Provisioning Services 7.0*. As you are reading this book, you have most likely heard about the virtual disk streaming solution from the Citrix system. In this chapter, we will thoroughly get acquainted with the topic, right from getting started with Citrix's provisioning service, features, and functionality, to terminology and system requirements for Citrix Provisioning Services 7.0.

In this chapter, we will cover:

- A background of Citrix Provisioning Services 7.0
- Architecture of Citrix Provisioning Services 7.0
- Terminology used in Citrix Provisioning Services
- System Requirements of Citrix Provisioning Services

The background of Citrix® Provisioning Services 7.0

Citrix Systems acquired the company Ardence based out of Virginia Beach, U.S. Ardence developed a product called Provisioning Services, which is now **Citrix Provisioning Service (PVS)**. Its primary functionality is to provision the disk via the software-streaming technology. The product aims to fulfill the needs of the administrator in provisioning and re-provisioning systems from a single shared-disk image. It can potentially completely eliminate the need of managing and patching individual servers and desktops. Instead, all the image and patch management is done on the single master image and replicated across the system.

The single master image will be called vDisk. The master image is configured, managed, and delivered from a centralized datacenter and consequently makes Citrix Provisioning Service increase security and flexibility and enables uncompromised user experiences.

Citrix Provisioning Services address the major problems of the IT business, such as **operational expenditure (opex)** and **capital expenditure (Cpex)**, along with the time spent on managing distributed servers, desktops, laptops, or kiosk-based devices. Usually, even the operational cost (opex) is higher than the server and system procurement cost. In order to overcome this major problem, Citrix came up with an out-of-the-box solution, transforming the existing IT relationship between hardware and the software that runs on the hardware, which also enables the organization to reduce the need for managing multiple disks even with the rapid growth of servers and desktops as well as providing the high efficiency of centralized distributed management.

Citrix Provisioning Service brings in higher benefits to server pool administrators and desktop pool administrators. For server pool administrators in the current trending IT infrastructure management, a majority of the servers are in need of unique patch compliances, but doing so is highly challenging in terms of technical and triple-factor constraints (Cost, Time, and Quality).To overcome this constraint, Provisioning Services' patch management for servers and desktops becomes highly reliable and secure. Patching is done on a single image, and it is streamed across systems on bootup. For desktop administrators, Citrix Provisioning Service helps in reducing the effort and cost involved in managing both the physical and virtual desktops. Provisioning helps to reduce storage cost (90 percent) to a huge extent for a desktop virtualization solution.

Citrix Provisioning Service comes in two different editions, which are Provisioning Services for datacenters and Provisioning Services for desktops.

In this book, we will be dealing with Citrix Provisioning Services 7.0. A lot of the known issues of the previous release have been fixed. To know the list of issues fixed, please refer to `http://support.citrix.com/product/provsvr/pvsv7.0/topic/fixedissue`.

High-level logical flow of Citrix® Provisioning Services

Citrix Provisioning Service can be used to convert the existing static deployment to dynamic deployment. vDisks are streamed to diskless desktops and servers on demand and not physically installed.

A high-level logical streaming flow with a three-step process is illustrated in the following figure:

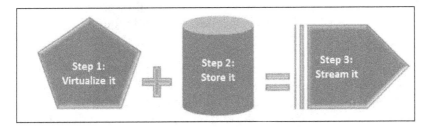

- **Virtualize it** means to create a master image with a desktop OS and applications
- **Store it** means to store the virtual image on a network storage device
- **Stream it** implies stream on demand from datacenters to diskless servers and desktops

Having understood this logical flow, let us move to the technical flow of Citrix Provisioning Services as illustrated in the following screenshot:

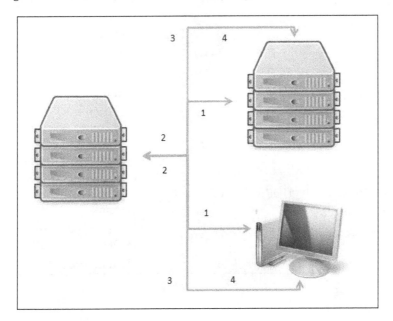

1. On-demand desktops and servers send a request for a vDisk to the provisioning server.

2. Citrix Provisioning Server sends a boot file back to the desktops and servers upon successful communication.

3. Based on the boot file configuration (desktops and servers boots) with respect to the configuration file, the vDisk is located and mounted on the Citrix Provisioning Server.

The application and the disk are streamed to the desktops and servers. It appears to the users like a real hard disk attached to the desktops and servers (target device). With an understanding of the technical flow of Citrix Provisioning Services, now let us look at the ports used in communication with the network in the following table:

Component	Protocol	Port series	Purpose
Provisioning server	UDP	6890 – 6909	Used for inter-server communication (Post 6.0 Version)
	UDP	6905 – 6909	Used for inter-server communication (Pre 6.0 Version)
	UDP	6910	Used for the desktop and server (target device) to logon to PVS
	UDP	6910 – 6930	Used for vDisk streaming
	UDP	6969	Used for boot from ISO/USB, in a short, two-stage boot (BDM)
	TCP	54321	SOAP service
	TCP	54321	SOAP service
Domain controller	TCP	389	Communication between target device and Active Directory
Microsoft SQL server	TCP	1433	Communication between PVS infrastructure and the SQL DB system
DHCP server [Broadcast]	UDP	67	Communication between PVS infrastructure and the DHCP system
PXE service [Broadcast]	UDP	67/4011	Used for bootstrap name in case of DHCP option 66
TFTP server	TCP	69	Used for bootstrap delivery

Architecture of Citrix® Provisioning Services 7.0

Citrix Provisioning Services is designed to connect to administrative roles within a Citrix Provisioning Services farm. A Citrix Provisioning Services administrator role is to govern the components an administrator can manage or view in the Citrix Provisioning Console. There are several components that make up a Citrix Provisioning Services farm.

The following diagram provides a high-level view of the basic Provisioning Services infrastructure and clarifies how Provisioning Services components might appear within the datacenter post installation and implementation:

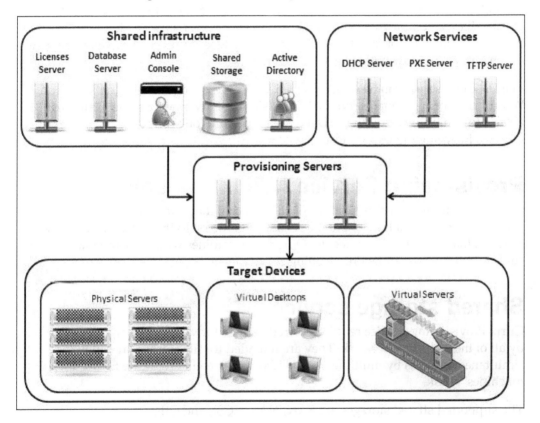

Provisioning Service License server

The License Server either should be installed within the shared infrastructure or an existing Citrix license server can be selected. However, we have to ensure the Provisioning Service license is configured in your existing Citrix Enterprise License servers.

A License Server can be selected when the Provisioning Service Configuration Wizard is run on a planned server. All Provisioning Servers within the farm must be able to communicate with the License Server.

Provisioning Service Database server

The database stores all system configuration settings that exist within a farm. Only one database can exist within a provisioning service farm. We can choose an existing SQL Server database or install an SQL Server in cluster for High Availability from a redundancy business continuities perspective.

The Database server can be selected when the Provisioning Service Configuration Wizard runs on a planned server. All Provisioning Servers within the farm must be able to communicate with the Database server, and only one database can exist within a Provisioning Service farm

Provisioning Service Admin Console

Citrix Provisioning Service Admin Console is a tool that is used to control your Provisioning Services implementation. After logging on to the console, we can select the farm that we want to connect to. Our role determines what we can look at in the console and operate in the Provisioning Service farm.

Shared storage service

Citrix Provisioning Service requires shared storage for vDisks that are accessible by all of the users in a network. They are intended for file storage and allowing simultaneous access by multiple users without the need to replicate files to their machines' vDisk.

The supported shared storages are SAN, NAS, iSCSI, and CIFS.

Active Directory Server

Citrix Provisioning service requires Microsoft's Active Directory. It provides authentication and authorization mechanisms as well as a framework, within which other related services can be deployed. Microsoft Active Directory is an LDAP-compliant database that contains objects. The most commonly used objects are users, computers, and groups

Network services

Dynamic Host Control Protocol (DHCP) is used for the purpose of getting IP addresses for servers and systems.

Trivial File Transfer Protocol (TFTP) is used for automated transfer of boot configuration files between servers and a system in a network.

Preboot Execution Environment (PXE) is a standard used for client/server interface that allows networked computers that boot remotely to boot locally instead.

Citrix® Provisioning Server

A Provisioning Server is a server that has stream services installed on it. The purpose is to stream software from vDisks on demand to the target devices. In a few implementations, vDisks exist directly on the Provisioning Server. In larger implementations, Citrix Provisioning Servers will get the vDisk from sharedstorage.

Citrix Provisioning Server also reclaims and provides configuration in sequence to and from the Provisioning Services Database. The Provisioning Server feature of configuration is available to ensure that there isHigh Availability and that load balancing is in place for target devices.

Terminology

Citrix uses a variety of terminology in this product. Now let us see the most important terms used in this product.

Citrix® Provisioning Service farms

A Citrix PVS farm represents the peak level of the Provisioning Services infrastructure on a console. The farm is formed when the Provisioning Services Configuration Wizard runs on the first Citrix Provisioning Server in the farm. It will be added to the farm as well. Farms provide a vDisk administrator with a method for operating all components within the farm, such as Farm properties, Active Directory configurations, product licensing, administrative roles, provisioning servers, vDisk images, sites, stores, views, target devices, and target device collections.

Citrix® Provisioning Service stores

The Citrix Provisioning Service store is a logical name that is assigned to a physical or virtual vDisk storage place. The store name is the common name used by all Citrix Provisioning Servers within the farm. A Citrix Provisioning Service farm contains one or more stores.

The Citrix Provisioning Service disk storage administration is very important because a Provisioning Server should have vDisks stored, and each vDisk can be more than a few gigabytes in volume. In the case of issues, our streaming performance can be improved by using the best storage solution instead.

Citrix® Provisioning Service sites

The first site for Citrix Provisioning Service is created with the Citrix Provisioning Configuration Wizard run on the first Provisioning Server in the farm. A site provides both a site administrator and farm administrator with a scheme of representing and operating its components within a site, which includes servers, vDisk pools, vDisk Update Management components, device collections, views, and hosts. Citrix Provisioning Service can have one or more sites live within a farm.

Citrix® Provisioning Service vDisk

Citrix Provisioning vDisks live on a Provisioning Server as disk image files or on-a shared-storage device within reach. A vDisk is available with a base image file in the VHD format and associated files, such as properties files (.pvp) and VHD differencing disks (.avhd). Post that, vDisks are assigned to target devices.

Citrix® Provisioning Service vDisk modes

Citrix Provisioning vDisks live on a Provisioning Server and can be configured in two different modes. One is the Private Image mode and the other, the Standard Image mode. The Private Image mode fulfills the read-and-write purpose for a single device (physical servers, virtual servers, and virtual desktops), whereas the Standard Image mode fulfills the read-only purpose for multiple devices (physical servers, virtual servers, and virtual desktops).

Citrix® Provisioning Service vDisk pools

Citrix Provisioning Service vDisk pools are gatherings of all vDisks available to a site. Citrix Provisioning Service allows you to have only one vDisk pool per site.

Citrix® Provisioning Service vDisk Update Management

The Citrix Provisioning Service vDisk Update Management attribute is used to configure the automation of vDisk updates using virtual machines. Robotically vDisk updates can take place on a scheduled base or on demand when the administrator initiates the update directly from the Console. The Citrix Provisioning Service vDisk feature updates are delivered from the **Electronic Software Delivery (ESD)** servers.

When you expand the console tree, the vDisk Update Management utility appears. On further expansion the vDisks and Tasks components appear.

Citrix® Provisioning Service write cache destination

Citrix Provisioning Services provides a number of write cache destination options, such as on the device's RAM, on the device's server disk, on the device's server persisted, on the device's hard drive, and on the device's hard drive persisted. These are described in the following table:

Device	Description
On the device RAM	The write cache can live as a temporary file in the target system device's RAM. It is fastest way of disk access, the reason being that memory access is always faster than disk access. But it only supports Windows 7 and Windows Server 2012.

Device	Description
On the device's disk	The write cache can live as a temporary file in NTFS format and is located in the target system's hard drive; this option does not require any additional software components.
On the device's disk persisted	The write cache can live as a temporary file in the target system's hard drive. It requires a different bootstrap, and hence it can be used for experimental purposes. It only supports NT6.1 or later versions.
On the device's PVS server disk	The write cache can live as a temporary file in Citrix Provisioning Server. In this option, writes are handled by the Provisioning Server, in turn increasing disk I/O and network traffic.
On the device's PVS server disk persisted	The write cache can live as a temporary file in the Citrix Provisioning Server. This cache option allows for the saving of changes between reboots even after the rebooting changes made can be read by the target devices. One of the two main benefits is that PVS saves the target device-specific changes that are made to the vDisk image, and the other one is the same as the standard vDisk image. Some disadvantages that are also observed are that the Cache files are not deleted and manual deletion of housekeeping is required periodically.

System requirements

Citrix Provisioning Service can be installed with following requirements:

Citrix Provisioning Server	
Requirement	**Description**
Operation system	Windows 2012: Standard, Essential, and Datacenter editions; Windows 2008 R2; Windows 2008 R2 SP1: Standard, Enterprise, and DataCenter editions; and all editions of Windows 2008 (32 or 64-bit)
Processor	Intel or AMD x86 or x64 compatible
	2 GHz / 3 GHz (preferred) / 3.5 GHz Dual Core / HT or an equal one for growing capacity fulfiller
Memory	2 GB RAM; 4 GB (greater than 250 vDisks)

Citrix Provisioning Server

Requirement	Description
Hard disk	To determine IOPS needed along RAID Level, please plan your sizing based on the following formula:
	Total Raw IOPS = Disk Speed IOPS x # of Disks
	Functional IOPS = ((Total Raw IOPS * Write %)/RAID Penalty) + (Total Raw IOPS*Read %)
	For more, please refer to `http://support.citrix.com/servlet/KbServlet/download/24559-102-647931/`
Network adapter	IP assignment to servers should be static. 1 GB is recommended for less than 250 target devices. If you are planning for more than 250 devices, Dual 1 GB is recommended. For High Availability, please have two NICs for redundancy purposes.
Pre-requisite software components	Microsoft .NET 4.0 and Microsoft Powershell 3.0 loaded on a fresh OS

The Infrastructure components required are described as follows:

Requirement	Description
Supported database	Microsoft SQL 2008, Microsoft SQL 2008 R2, and Microsoft SQL 2012 Server (32-bit or 64-bit editions) databases can be used for the Provisioning ServicesDB sizing. Please refer to `http://msdn.microsoft.com/en-us/library/ms187445.aspx`. For HA Planning, please refer to `http://support.citrix.com/proddocs/topic/provisioning-7/pvs-install-task1-plan-6-0.html`.
Supported hypervisor	XenServer 6.0, Microsoft SCVMM 2012 SP1 with Hyper-V 3.0; SCVMM 2012 with Hyper-V 2.0, VMware ESX 4.1, ESX 5, or ESX 5 Update 1; vSphere 5.0, 5.1, 5.1 Update 1; along with Physical Devices for 3D Pro Graphics (Blade Servers, Windows Server OS machines, and Windows Desktop OS machines with XenDesktop VDA installed).

Requirement	Description
Provisioning Console	**Hardware requirement**: Processor 2 GHz, Memory 2 GB ,Hard Disk 500 MB
	Supported Operating Systems: all editions of Windows Server 2008 (32-bit or 64- bit); Windows Server 2008 R2: Standard, DataCenter, and Enterprise editions; Windows Server 2012: Standard, Essential, and Datacenter editions; Windows 7 (32-bit or 64-bit); Windows XP Professional (32-bit or 64-bit); Windows Vista (32-bit or 64-bit): Business, Enterprise, and Ultimate (retail licensing); and all editions of Windows 8 (32-bit or 64-bit).
	Pre-Requisite Software: MMC 3.0, Microsoft .NET 4.0, and Windows PowerShell 2.0
	In case we are using Provisioning Services, we would require XenDesktop and, NET 3.5 SP1, and in the event that we are using Provisioning Services then we would require SCVMM 2012 SP1 and PowerShell 3.0.
Supported ESD	Apply only in case VDisk Update Management is used; ESD supports WSUS Server-3.0 SP2 and Microsoft System Center Configuration Management 2007 SP2, 2012, and 2012 SP1
Supported target device	**Supported Operating Systems**: all editions of Windows 8 (32 or 64-bit); Windows 7 SP1 (32 bits or 64 bits): Enterprise, Professional, and Ultimate (Support alone in Private Mode); Windows XP Professional SP3 32-bit and Windows XP Professional SP2 64-bit; Windows Server 2008 R2 SP1: Standard, DataCenter, and Enterprise editions; Windows Server 2012: Standard, Essential, and Datacenter editions.

Summary

In this chapter, we learned about getting started with Citrix Provisioning Service, the product overview, essentials of products, the features fulfilling the real-world needs, the logical flow of the product, the technical architecture of the product, the terminology, and the system requirements for installing for Provisioning Service. In the upcoming chapter, we will learn about the installation of Provisioning Service.

2
Installing and Configuring Citrix® Provisioning Services 7.0

With the knowledge gained in *Chapter 1, Introduction to Citrix® Provisioning Services 7.0*, you will have an overview of Citrix Provisioning Services, and have understood the architecture and terminology used. Following which you also learned the system requirements to set up provisioning services in your infrastructure. Now, let us look at the step-by-step procedure to install Citrix Provisioning Server and Citrix Provisioning Console using a GUI and command-line interface, followed by configuring Citrix Provisioning components.

In this chapter, we will learn:

- Citrix Provisioning Server installation using GUI and command-line interface
- Citrix Provisioning Console installation
- Configuring Citrix Provisioning components
- Configuring Citrix Provisioning components using command-line interface

Installing Citrix® Provisioning Server using GUI

To get started with the installation of the Provisioning Server, first and foremost, get the software source in place. To do so, please download the Citrix Provisioning ISO from `http://www.citrix.com/downloads.html`.

Map the ISO image to the planned server. UNP is not supported. The operating system needs to be one of the following to ensure support:

- All editions of Windows Server 2008 (32- or 64-bit)
- Windows Server 2008 R2
- Windows Server 2008 R2 SP1: Standard, Enterprise, and Datacenter editions
- Windows Server 2012: Standard, Essential, and Datacenter editions

Along with that, please cross check that the OS is patched up to the standard level with Windows patches and performs equivalent tests to ensure that the updates are supported.

To perform the installation using a GUI, please perform the following steps:

1. From your ISO, run `PVS_Server.exe`.
2. On your screen, the **Provisioning Services** wizard appears. Click on **Server Installation** as shown in the following screenshot:

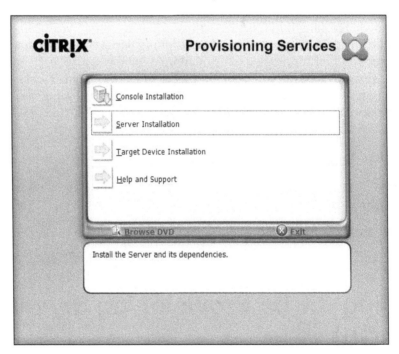

3. On your screen, please select **Install Server**:

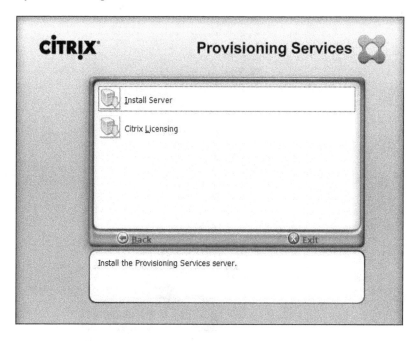

On selecting **Install Server**, the prerequisites shown in the following screenshot will be installed for Windows Server 2012:

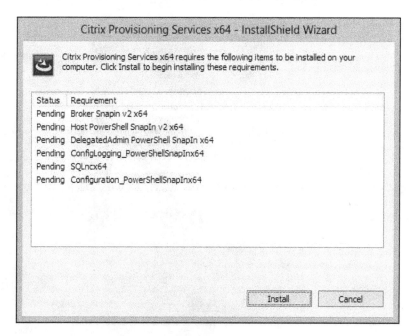

4. On your screen, a Citrix Provisioning Services welcome message appears. Read the agreement fully and in the end click on **Next**:

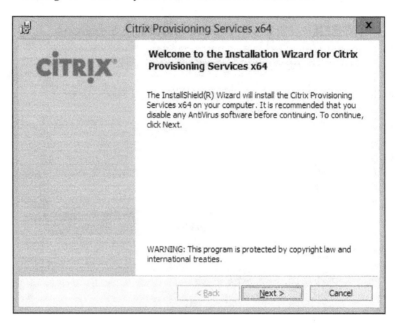

5. Citrix product license agreement appears on the screen. Read the agreement fully and click on **Next**:

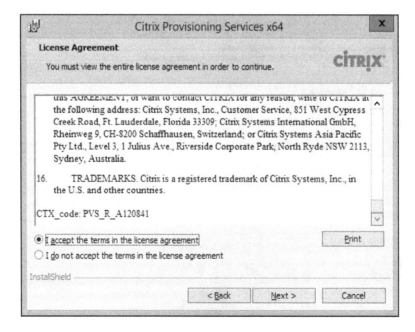

6. This step is optional. Provide the customer and organization names in appropriate textboxes, as can be seen in the following screenshot, and click on **Next**:

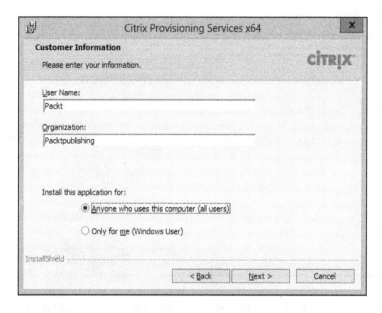

7. On your screen, click on **Change**. Then enter the folder name or navigate to the required folder where the Provisioning Services program should be installed, or leave it default, and then click on **Next**:

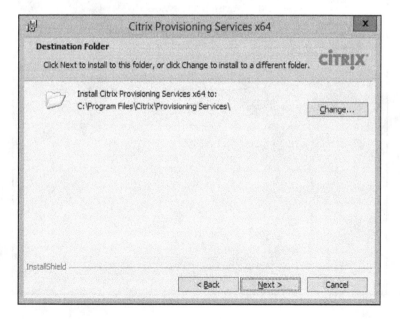

8. Now go ahead and click on **Install** as shown in the following screenshot:

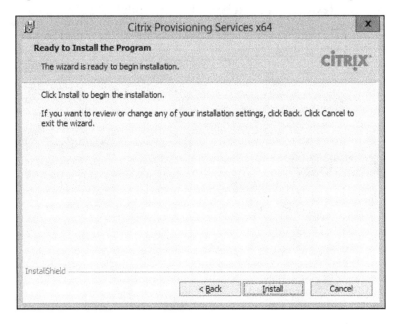

9. Upon selecting **Install**, a message appears on the screen to indicate the installation is in progress. Post successful installation of all the components, a completed message appears as shown in the following screenshot:

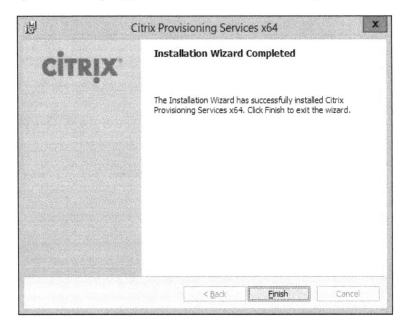

10. On your screen, click on **Finish** to complete the installation of Citrix Provisioning Services. Now, the configuring wizard will open automatically.

We will stop here, before we start configuring Provisioning Services. Now let us look at silent installation.

Installing Citrix® Provisioning Services using the command-line interface

To silently install Citrix Provisioning Server, in case you perform a default installation, please use the following command:

```
<Installer Name>.exe /s /v"/qn"
```

In case you use a different destination for silent installation of Citrix Provisioning Server, please use the following command:

```
<Installer Name>.exe /s /v"/qn INSTALLDIR=X: \Destination"
```

In case you have planned your infrastructure with high availability, just go ahead and repeat the installation on your other node. Post installation, while performing a configuration, ensures you select your site name and server name. While providing the server name, ensure the maximum length is 15 characters and not beyond that. Please do not entrain for FQDN on the completion to verify that you have added Provisioning Servers to the site. When you go to the console, the added server is visible.

Installing Citrix® Provisioning Services Console 7.0 using GUI

Before we begin with the Provisioning Services Console installation on the planned server, we strongly recommend you to ensure that the operating system is patched and compatible. Only the following operating systems such as all editions of Windows Server 2008 (64- or 32-bit), Windows Server 2008 R2, Windows Server 2008 R2 SP1: Standard, Enterprise, and Datacenter editions, Windows Server 2012: Standard, Essential, and Datacenter editions, Windows XP Professional (32 or 64-bit), Windows 7 (64-bit or 32-bit), all editions of Windows 8 (64-bit or 32-bit), and Windows Vista (32 or 64-bit) are compatible. During the Provisioning Services Console installation, the boot device management tool is also installed.

To install, please perform the following steps:

1. Go to the ISO map folder and run `PVS_Console.exe`.

2. On your screen, a Provisioning Services welcome message appears.
    Click on **Next**:

3. Next, the Citrix product license agreement appears on your screen. Read the
    agreement completely, go to the end, and click on **Next**:

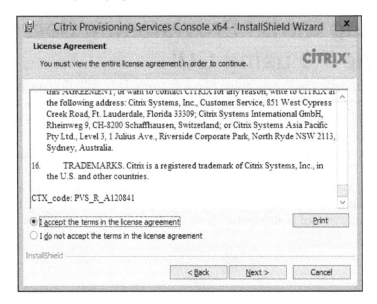

4. On your screen, provide the customer name and organization name in appropriate textboxes, and then click on **Next**:

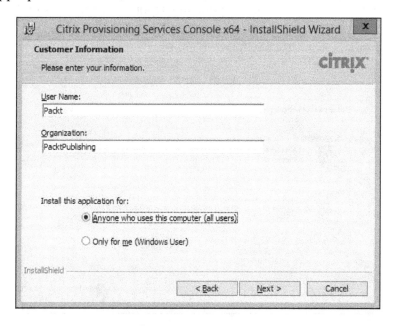

5. On your screen, click on **Change**. Enter the folder name or navigate to the required folder where the Provisioning Services should be installed or leave it default and then click on **Next**:

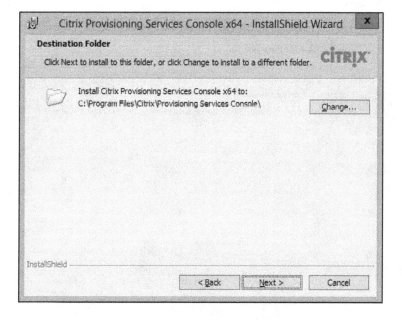

6. Choose the appropriate radio button, either **Complete** (default installation of all the components) or **Custom** (option to select which components to install and where to install those components). Upon selection, click on **Next**:

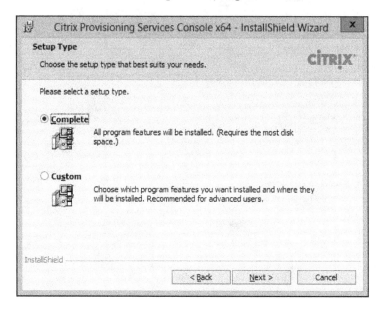

7. If you selected **Complete**, the message, **Ready to Install the Program**, appears. If you selected **Custom**, choose the required component that you planned to install, and then click on **Install**:

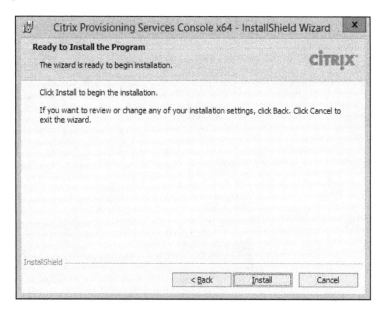

8. On the screen, the message installation in progress appears, and post successful installation of all the components, a completed message appears.

9. On your screen, click on **Finish** to complete the installation of Citrix Provisioning Console:

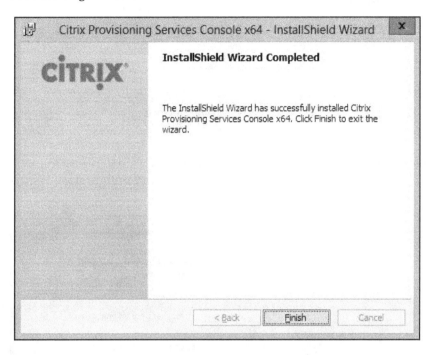

In case you are planning to upgrade from the previous version of the Citrix Provisioning Console, in place upgrade is not supported. Please remove the previous version completely and perform a fresh installation.

Configuring Citrix® Provisioning Server 7.0

In the final step, during the installation of the Provisioning Server, the configuration wizard will appear on screen. We paused at this topic earlier, now let us resume from there. During this initial stage of configuration, configuration logs are located under `C:\ProgramData\Citrix\Provisioning Services` (on Windows Server 2008) and `C:\Documents and Settings\All Users\Application Data\Citrix\Provisioning Services` (on Windows 2003) by default.

The following are core components that need to be configured based on the configuration wizard. Before you start the real-world implementation of the Provisioning Server, I would recommend you to plan for future scaling as well:

- Configure the network topology
- Configure the farm
- Configure the database
- Configure the site
- Configure the license server
- Configure network cards for the stream service
- Configure the bootstrap server

In case you cancelled the configuration wizard, to reinitiate it, please follow the given navigation. Launch **Citrix Provisioning Services Configuration Wizard** from **All Programs**:

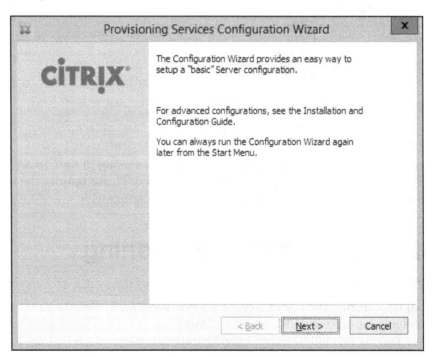

To begin with the Citrix Provisioning Server configuration, start with the configuration of the network topology. It is a two-step process, where the first step is to select the network service to provide IP addresses. To assign the target with the IP address, during configuration we are allowed to use the existing network as well:

1. In case you are installing PVS on DHCP, select the radio button against DHCP on this server, and then choose any one of the following mechanisms:

   ○ Microsoft DHCP

   ○ Provisioning Services' BOOTP service, other BOOTP service, or DHCP service

   Select your planned option and then click on **Next** and in case DHCP does not run on this server, select the radio button next to **The service that runs on another computer** and then click on **Next**:

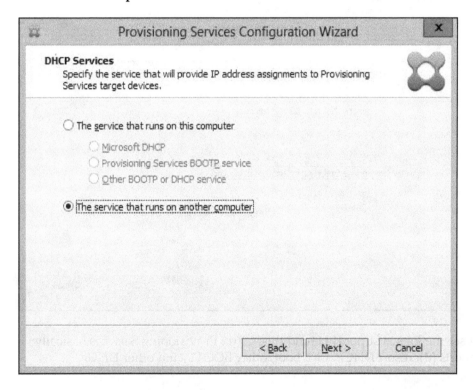

2. Next, choose the network service to provide the PXE boot information. During this configuration, we need to ensure that the target system is allowed to download the boot configuration file from the TFTP server. If the PXE service is running on this server, select the service that runs on this computer, and select one of the following mechanisms:

   ° Microsoft DHCP

   ° Provisioning Services' PXE service.

   If this server does not provide the PXE boot information, select **The service that runs on another computer** and click on **Next**:

Just see the logical support behind this. Citrix Provisioning Services basically supports Microsoft DHCP, PXE boot, other BOOTP, and other DHCP.

The next step in the Provisioning Services configuration is to configure the Citrix Provisioning Services farm. The farm can be configured in two ways; one is creating the farm and another one is joining the existing farm, by performing the following steps:

1. To create a farm, in the configuration wizard, on the **Farm Configuration** window, select **Create farm** and click on **Next**:

2. Choose the **Browse** button for the existing SQL DB name and instance name in the existing DB. Provide the SQL DB name and instance name.

    A failover option is also provided in the configuration wizard. To enable the failover option, choose the **Browse** button for the database mirror fail over option. Provide the SQL DB name and instance name in the existing DB and click on **Next**. This is the procedure to create a farm.

    Now let us look at the procedure to join an existing farm:

    1. On the **Farm Configuration** window, select **Join existing farm** and click on **Next**. Choose the **Browse** button to provide the appropriate SQL DB name and instance name in the existing DB.

    2. Once the farm name is displayed, please select the appropriate farm.

3. A failover option is also provided in the configuration wizard. To enable the failover option, choose the **Browse** button for the **Specify database mirror failover partner** option. Provide the SQL DB name and instance name in the existing DB and click on **Next**:

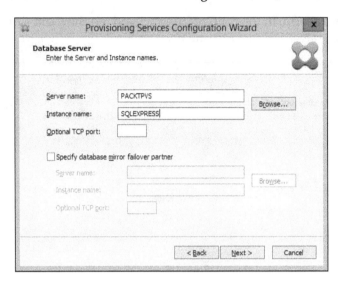

3. The next step in the Provisioning Services configuration is to configure the database. As you know, only one database exists within a farm to perform, so choose the database location (applies only if the database is not selected). On the **Database Server** window, click on **Browse** to open the SQL Servers and from the list of SQL Servers, choose the name of the server where this database exists and the instance to use, and then click on **Next**:

4. The next step is to configure the site. To do so, provide the site name. Refer to the preceding screenshot, where PACKT_Site is entered in the textbox. Provide a default path for **New Store** and click on **Next**:

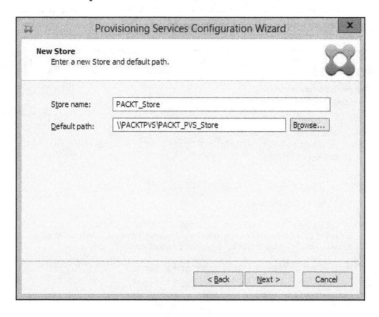

5. After this, we can configure the license server. Provide the name of the license server host and port number 27000, post configuration, validate license server communication with the Provisioning Server, and click on **Next**:

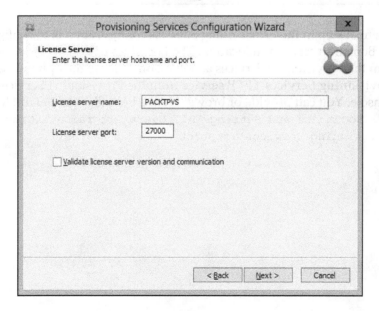

6. After this, we will configure network cards for stream and management consumption. Choose the appropriate card to be used for streaming and provide a **First communications port** number that will be used for the network communication (6890). Ensure that you provide a **Console port** number (54321) as well and click on **Next**:

7. The final step in the Provisioning Services configuration is to configure the Bootstrap server and location. The Bootstrap option can be configured from the Provisioning Services action menu. Choose the option **Use the Provisioning Services TFTP service** from the Provisioning Services Console. You can provide or browse for the boot file. The default location is C:\Documents and Settings\All Users\ProgramData\Citrix\ Provisioning Services\Tftpboot.

If a previous version of Provisioning Services was installed on this server, the default location will be: `C:\Program Files\Citrix\Provisioning Services\TftpBoot`.

We must run the configuration wizard to modify the default location to `C:\Documents and Settings\All Users\ProgramData` or `ApplicationData\Citrix\Provisioning Services\Tftpb` and we can also choose Provisioning Servers for the boot process. To do so, please use the **Add** button.

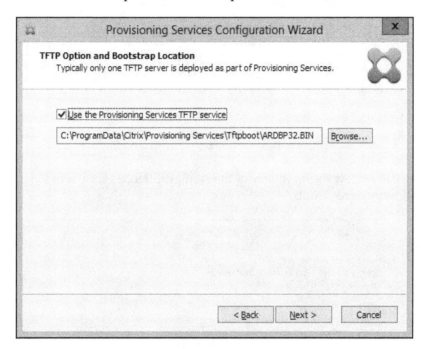

Upon configuring the TFTP service, the subsequent step is to configure the bootstrap network identification. Configure the server IP, server port, server subnet mask, and server default gateway.

For Enterprise, you can configure bootstrap on high availability. Following which you can perform advanced configuration for the features mentioned in the following screenshot:

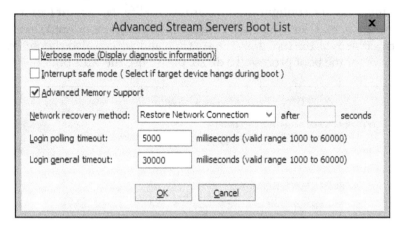

We can review the summary of the configuration, as shown in the following screenshot:

8. Finally, once done, you can click on **Finish**:

On successful configuration, the wizard will return the following screen:

Configuring Provisioning Services using the command-line interface

In order to run the configuration wizard from the command-line interface, for easy administration and to fulfill multiple server installation, follow this three-step process:

1. First, get the `ConfigWizard.answer` file from the server already installed.
2. Next, change the IP address on the `ConfigWizard.answer` file.
3. The last step is to copy the next server, where the PVS needs to be configured and then run the `ConfigWizard.exe` file with the `/a` parameter.

The procedure for configuring answer files using `ConfigWizard.exe` is as follows:

1. On a configured Provisioning Server, execute the `ConfigWizard.exe` file using the `/s` parameter.
2. On the **Farm Configuration** screen, opt for the option **Join existing farm**.
3. Go ahead with the default configuration settings for the rest of the screen, and click on **Finish**.
4. Copy the resultant `ConfigWizard.ans` file from the Provisioning Services source directory. The location of the folder may vary as listed:
    - If it is Windows Server 2003, go to `\Documents and Settings\All Users\Application Data\Citrix\Provisioning Services`.
    - If it is Windows Server 2008 or Windows Server 2008 R2, go to `ProgramData\Citrix\Provisioning Services`.

You can run the `ConfigWizard.exe` file via a silent installation as follows:

To configure servers, run the `ConfigWizard.exe` file with the `/a` parameter on each server that needs to be configured and get a list of valid `ConfigWizard` parameters:

1. Run `ConfigWizard.exe` with the `/?` parameter.
2. In the Provisioning Services' `Application Data` directory, open the resulting `ConfigWizard.out` file.
3. Scroll down to the bottom of the file to view all valid parameters.

To get the list of valid `ConfigWizard` commands with descriptions, follow these steps:

1. Run the `ConfigWizard.exe` file with the `/c` parameter.
2. In the Provisioning Services' `Application Data` directory, open the resulting `ConfigWizard.out` file.
3. Scroll down to the bottom of the file to view all valid parameters.

Summary

In this chapter, we have learned about installing and configuring Citrix Provisioning Services, Citrix Provisioning Services Console using a graphical user interface and using the command-line interface. In the upcoming chapter, we will learn about management of the Citrix Provisioning disk.

3
Managing Citrix®
Provisioning Disk

With the knowledge gained in *Chapter 2, Installation and Configuring Citrix® Provisioning Services 7.0,* you would have understood the procedure to install Provisioning Services and the steps involved in the installation of Provisioning Server Console, along with detailed configuration of the same. In this chapter, we will learn about organizing a (master) principal target device aimed at imaging, constructing a vDisk image, creating a vDisk, allocating vDisk to target disk, and dealing with bootstrap files and booting devices.

In this chapter, we will cover the following topics:

- Organizing a (master) principal target device
- Allocating vDisk to target disk
- Dealing with bootstrap files and booting devices

Organizing a principal target device

Post installation and configuration of Provisioning Services and Console, the next step to follow is all about organizing a (master) principal target device aimed for imaging. In order to do so, we have to follow a four-step process, which is as follows:

1. Checking the readiness of the (master) principal target device's hard disk.
2. Configuring (master) principal target device's BIOS settings.
3. Configuring server network adapter BIOS settings.
4. Deploying the master target device application and other updates.

Checking the readiness of the master target device's hard disk

The (master) principal target device's hard disk is not a target device. This particular hard disk should be imaged to the respective vDisk. On completion of imaging, the hard disk can be detached from the (master) principal target device on demand.

Multiple target devices that share a single vDisk, components such as motherboard, network card, and video card should be identical across all. However, Citrix Provisioning Services still support different vendor components as well.

Before we configure a master target device, it is essential to create a new vDisk, which is done via an imaging wizard.

Please ensure that Windows automount is allowed and Windows autoplay is deactivated. Also, ensure sufficient space is available in the vDisk store, and one more final mandatory requirement is to make a note of which NIC is used for the imaging process. The process is as follows:

1. On the master target device, go to the Citrix folder , look for the **Provisioning Services** folder and open **Imaging Wizard**.

2. A welcome screen is displayed. Click on **Next**.

3. Click on **Next** once the **Connect to Farm** screen appears. Provide the server name or IP address of a Citrix Provisioning Server within the farm.

4. Provide the Windows credentials and now click on **Next**:

5. On the next screen, the **Microsoft Volume Licensing** screen appears. Select the volume license option to use for target devices or select **None** if volume licensing is not being used or choose one of the following options:

   ○ **Key Management Service (KMS)**

   ○ **Multiple Activation Key (MAK)**

6. Create a new vDisk, or use an existing vDisk by providing the vDisks' name, and click on **Next**.

7. Upon the selection of a new vDisk, the following information is required to be updated:

   ○ Name of the vDisk

   ○ Choose the store wherever vDisk exists, and the vDisk format from the appropriate drop-down menus.. In case of VHD, the format is **Dynamic** and the **Block size** value should be within 2 MB or 16 MB. Click on **Next**.

○ Define the volume size on the **Configure Volume** screen and now click on **Next**.

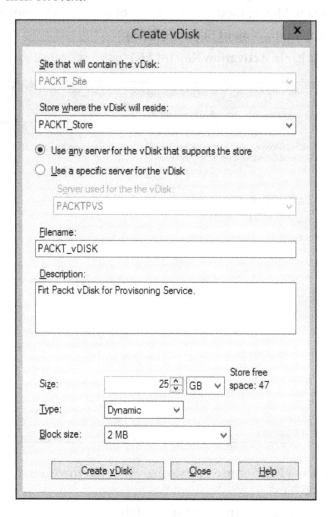

8. The **Add Target Device** screen appears. Provide the target device name and the MAC addresses associated with one of the NICs, if it is already a member of the farm. The existing target device will appear on the screen. Click on **Next**.

9. The summary screen appears. Verify all the options and click on **Finish**.

10. Click on **Yes** on the confirmation message to start the imaging process.

Post installation of the vDisk, the next step is to install the required components that need be deployed on the (master) principal target device, which are as follows:

- Install the Windows operating system
- Install the device drivers required
- Install Windows service packs updates
- Install the target device agent software
- Install your any application (optional)

The principal target device's BIOS configuration

During this phase, we will learn about the BIOS configuration of the target device. In order to do this, configure the principal target devices' BIOS settings and the BIOS extensions that are delivered by the network adapter.

Different servers will have their own BIOS setup interfaces (please follow the respective vendor guide). The BIOS settings can be performed with the help of following steps:

1. Get into the BIOS of the server and set the network adapter with the PXE option enabled.
2. Save and exit with changes made in the system BIOS.
3. To assign vDisk to the target device, please ensure that the target device is set to boot from its hard drive over the network.

Server network adapter BIOS configuration

Once the (master) principal target device's bios configuration is done, the next step is to configure the target devices' system BIOS settings, in order to boot from the network device as the top most priority followed by a local device. Different systems have their own BIOS setup (please follow the respective vendor guide):

1. Boot the system and get into the BIOS of the target device and modify the boot order. The network device has to be booted first, followed by the local device.
2. Save and exit with changes made in the system BIOS.

Deploying the master target device application and operating system updates

Once the server network adapter's BIOS configuration is done, the next step is to deploy the (master) principal target device application and OS updates. For this, we need to perform the following steps:

1. Boot the (master) principal target device from the local disk.

2. Ensure that all applications are not opened. If so, please close it.

3. Once you execute the appropriate installer, the installation window appears. Post mapping the ISO file, please execute the application.

4. On the next screen, select **Target Device Installation**:

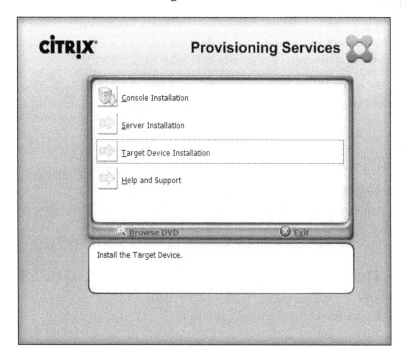

5. In the wizard screen, select the **Target Device Installation** and wait for the Provisioning Services wizard to start:

6. On the screen now, you would have got a welcome message. Please read the message and click on **Next**:

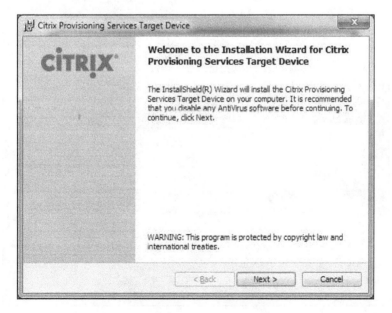

7. On the screen, read the license agreement completely and click on **Next**:

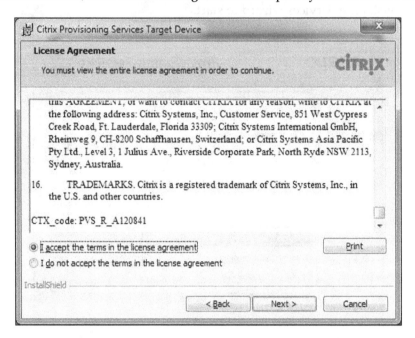

8. Now you can provide your own username and association name in the respective textboxes and choose the respective install user option:

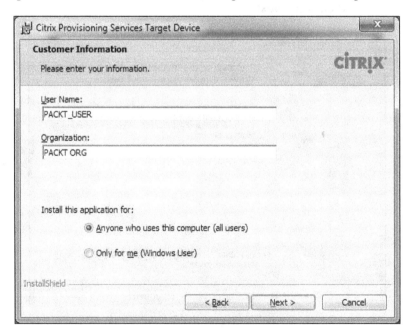

9. Now, click on **Next** in order to install the target device. By default, the path **C:\Program Files\Citrix\Provisioning Services** will be displayed. Optionally, click on **Change** to modify the location of the installation. Once the respective path is selected, click on **Next**:

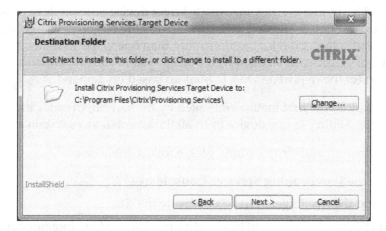

10. Now, to start the installation, click on the **Install** button. The installation status information is shown in the wizard:

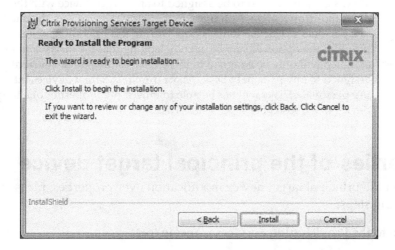

The installation wizard completion message is exhibited in the wizard when required components have been successfully installed.

11. Reboot the device upon successful completion of installation and start building the vDisk image.

Allocating a vDisk to the target device

In order to assign a vDisk to a single target disk, feature enabling can be performed using the method attached in the following section.

The process of assigning a vDisk to a single target device or to all devices within a target device collection is allowed, whereas outside the target, device collection is not allowed. In case, a target device requires more than one vDisk assigned to the target system, a list of vDisks will be displayed during system startup, which allows the end user to select the required vDisk to boot up based on demand.

Now, let us explore the first method followed by the second, in order use the drag-and-drop feature either to one device or to all the target devices within a collection.

To perform the drag-and-drop feature, please follow these steps:

1. Go to the **Provisioning Services Console** tree.

2. Expand the tree to get **vDisk Pool** inside the site.

3. Left-click on the vDisk and hold the mouse followed by dragging-and-dropping the vDisk option onto the target device or collection.

> vDisks are not allowed to be assigned to any target device with the drag-and-drop feature. Condition to that target device was allocated to a personal vDisk via XenDesktop. During this operation, a message provides the option to stay by acknowledging that the vDisk actually assigned will only be assigned to those devices that are not currently assigned to any personal vDisk. Apart from this, target devices that use personal vDisks will not be able to inherit the properties of a target device that doesn't use a personal vDisk.

Properties of the principal target device

To perform the principal target device modification over properties, please perform the following steps:

1. Go to the **Provisioning Services Console** tree.

2. Expand the **Device Collections** folder and then click on the collection folder where this target device is a member:

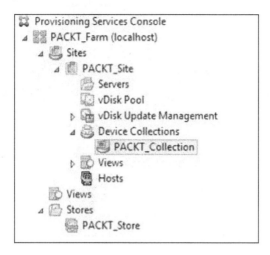

3. Now go ahead and right-click on the target device, and then choose **Properties**. The **Target Device Properties** screen should appear:

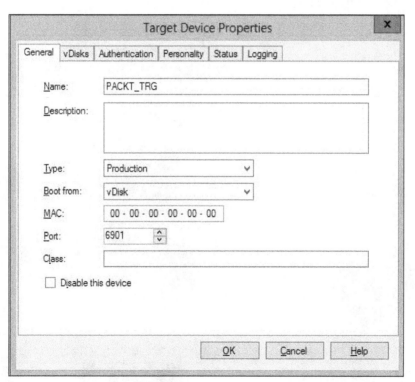

4. The **Target Device Properties** section starts with a **General** tab. Choose a boot method from the **Boot from** drop-down list that your target device should use:

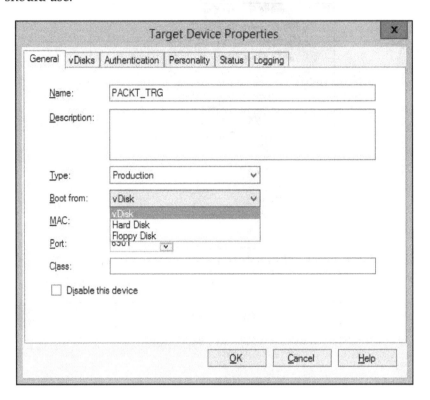

5. Now, move over to the **vDisks** tab, which is next to the **General** tab and under **vDisks** for this device section, choose the **Add** button. The assigned vDisks screen should appear:

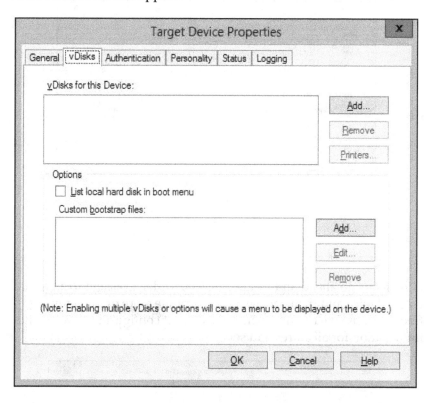

6. Click on **Add** to assign vDisks, and provide a store and server name in the drop-down menus:

7. Now let us go ahead and locate vDisks in order to assign to a particular target device and then choose an appropriate store or server using filter options. We can also admit the default configuration, which holds information for all stores and servers:

8. Choose the vDisks from the list, highlight the vDisks to allocate, click on **OK**, and then once again click on **OK** to save and close the **Target Device Properties** screen.

Dealing with the bootstrap files and boot devices

Managing a bootstrap file can be performed using two methods, which are as follows:

- To configure bootstrap via Provisioning Services Console
- To configure bootstrap via manage the boot devices utility

To perform bootstrap configuration via the Provisioning Services Console, please perform the following steps:

1. Go to **Citrix Provisioning Services Console** from the **Start** menu.

2. In the console window, select your planned Provisioning Server under the **Servers** folder, right-click on your planned Provisioning Server, and then select the **Configure Bootstrap...** option.

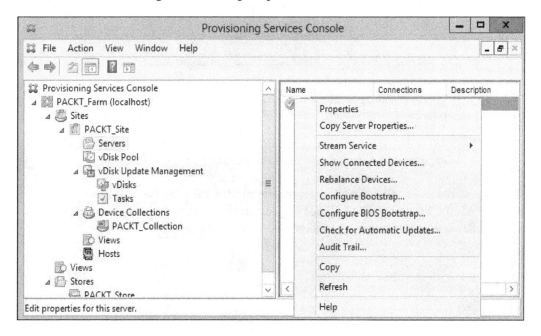

3. In the **Configure Bootstrap** screen, select the boot file which was copied to the `folder/shared` path that was selected during the **Provisioning Server** installation. The wizard will always pull the server that yields the list of bootstrap files from Provisioning Services `X:\ProgramData`. Ensure that the provisioning server is up and running to perform the bootstrap configuration:

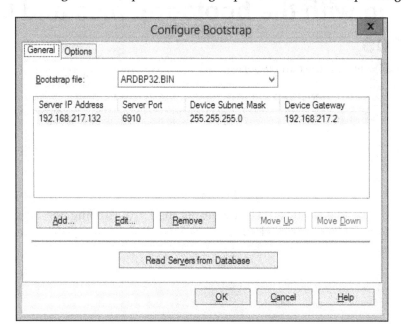

 In case you are planning to do an in place upgrade from the older version of Provisioning Services, then of course you must change the default location from `C:\Program Files\Citrix\Provisioning Services` to `C:\Documents and Settings\All Users\Application Data\Citrix\Provisioning Services\Tftpboot`.

The reason behind performing the preceding modification is that if it is not performed, the bootstrap file will not appear on the wizard and target devices will fail to book, with an error message saying missing TFTP.

If you have installed the Citrix Provisioning Console on a remote machine, choose the path of the remote Provisioning Server:

1. On clicking on the configuration wizard, it writes a list of IP addresses to the database for the server. Selecting **Read Servers from Database** gets the first IP address and port for the server and populates it into the list. This step should only be performed when the list is blank, or to replace the whole list with new values. These values are set in the streaming network cards section of the configuration wizard's network communications page. Provisioning Services uses the first network card selected:

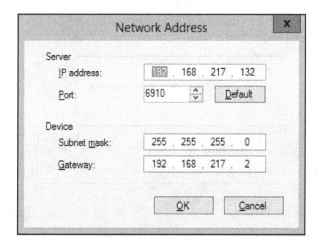

2. Choose from the following options:
   - Checking the **Verbose Mode** option helps to monitor the boot procedure over the target device. It allows system messaging over the target device.
   - Checking the **Interrupt safe mode** option helps in case the target device fails during the boot procedure.
   - Checking the **Advanced Memory Support** option (by default it is enabled) always aids to permit the bootstrap to work with brand new Windows OS as well.

You uncheck and disable this setting for the following cases:

- Windows XP or Windows Server OS 32-bit versions that do not support physical address extension.
- If your target device is lifeless or behaving unsteadily in early boot phase.

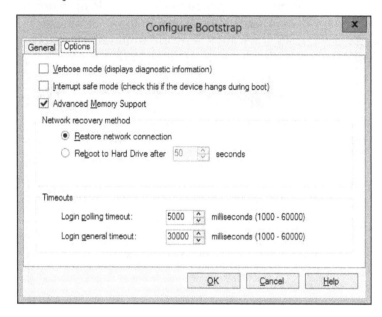

3. Choose from the given options of the network recovery mode:

   ○ Restoring the **Network Connections** mode option always aids in establishing a connection between the target device and Provisioning Server.

   ○ Rebooting to the **Hard Drive** mode option always aids the target device to undergo hardware asset restart, in case connection between the target device and provisioning service fails to reestablish, for the specified time of interval. Users are allowed to fix time intervals to wait even prior to rebooting. By default, the interval is set to 50 seconds.

All boot services such as PXE and TFTP should be in the identical IP/NIC stream service. This service is allowed to stay on the dissimilar IP/NIC. It also allows us to bind to different IP/NIC.

In case a partition containing the vDisks, which is formatted via an FAT filesystem-formatting mechanism, please reformat the disk using the NTFS filesystem-formatting mechanism. Citrix always recommends performing NTFS formatting for vDisks that contains a partition.

4. Login polling and general configuration can be performed based on the following parameters:

   ° **Login polling timeout**: The allowed range is from 1,000 to 60,000 milliseconds. Plan and provide the time, in milliseconds, among retries during polling for servers. Each server is sent a login request packet in a sequence. The first server that responds is consumed. This timeout is defined by how often to retry a single accessible server with an early login request. This timeout expresses how quickly the round-robin routine will switch from one server to another server available, to obtain the active server.

   ° **Login general timeout**: The allowed range is from 1,000 to 60,000 ms. Provide the timeout, in milliseconds, for all login interconnected to packets, excluding the initial login polling timeout.

In order to save your changes, click on **OK**.

Bootstrap configuring via the option **Manage boot devices utility**, provides an optional method to supply IP and boot information to target devices. This is completely an alternative solution compared to a traditional DHCP, PXE, or TFTP.

PXE is all about servers or systems that boot using a network interface self-sufficiently from remote data storage devices. The PXE protocol is a mixture of DHCP and TFTP.

Trivial File Transfer Protocol (TFTP) is a file transfer protocol that is noticeable for its easiness. Generally used for automated transfer of configuration or boot files between systems in a local environment. Comparing over FTP, TFTP is extremely limited, providing no authentication, and is rarely used interactively by a user.

Using methods such as TFTP/DHCP/PXE, the target device initializes, to obtain boot evidence straight away from the boot device. On gathering the required configuration evidence, the target device is able to locate and communicate. Along with that, it boots from the suitable Provisioning Server. Upon successful user authentication, the Provisioning Server offers vDisk to the target device with its authentication. Boot devices such as the following are supported: USB, CD-ROM, and hard disk partition.

The steps that are used to configure bootstrap via the Provisioning Service Console are listed as follows. The same step can be repeated, while you are planning to use the BDM utility:

1. Go to the **Start** menu on the Window Server and launch the **Boot Device Management** Tool.

2. Provide the server either using a DHCP name or with static IP:

3. Upon providing the server lookup, perform general and optional operations as planned:

4. After selecting the protocol and login option, the **Burn the Boot Device** screen would appear:

5. Choose the appropriate device with IP address, either DHCP or static, with the domain name. Choose the network planned and click on **Burn** to complete the BDM configuring.

6. After the boot target device configuration is complete, provide the system's BIOS configuration. Above the boot structure, bring the target device to the top -most position above all other boot devices. Save and exit with changes made and boot the system target device.

Summary

In this chapter, we have learned about organizing a (master) principal target device aimed at imaging, constructing vDisk image, creating vDisk, allocating vDisk to the target disk, followed by dealing with bootstrap files and booting devices. In the upcoming chapter, we will learn about operating Citrix Provisioning Services.

4
Operating Citrix® Provisioning Services 7.0

With the knowledge gained in *Chapter 3, Managing Citrix® Provisioning Disk*, you would have understood about Citrix Provisioning Services, organizing a principal (master) target device for imaging, allocating vDisk to a target disk, and dealing with bootstrap files and booting devices. In this chapter, we will learn about managing and operating farms, sites, stores, target devices, target device collection, Provisioning Server, views, and creating a vDisk.

In this chapter, we will cover the following topics:

- Managing and operating a farm
- Managing and operating sites
- Managing and operating stores
- Managing and operating the target device
- Managing and operating target device collection
- Managing views
- Managing and operating Provisioning Server
- Operating vDisks

Managing and operating a farm

A **farm** represents the topmost hierarchy of a Provisioning Service's infrastructure. Farms provide an administrator with a method to signify logical groups of Provisioning Service's components within sites.

All sites within a farm share that farm's Microsoft SQL database. A farm also includes a Citrix License Server, local or shared storage, along with a collection of target devices. As you know now what a farm is all about, let us see how to connect to a farm. In order to connect to a farm, please perform the following steps:

1. Right-click on **Provisioning Services Console** at the top of the tree and then choose **Connect to Farm**. This will open the following screenshot:

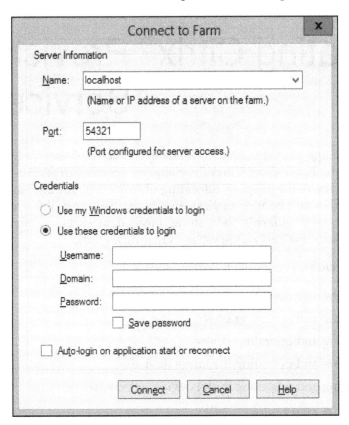

2. A wizard opens, asking for server information. Provide the server name or IP address of a provisioning streaming server in the **Name** section and the port configured for server access, which is **54321** by default.

3. Under the **Credentials** section, use the following options:

    ° Use the Windows credentials that you are currently logged in with.

    ° Use different Windows credentials by providing the **Username**, **Password**, and **Domain** values associated with those credentials. Optionally enable the **Save password** option and the auto-login feature to login automatically. When Console is opened, click on **Connect**. As a result, the Provisioning Service farm and tree appear in the Console tree.

Once you're connected to the Citrix Provisioning Service farm, it is time for us to explore the properties of the Provisioning Service farm.

In order to get the properties of the farm, right-click on the farm and choose **Properties**. By default, it shows the **General** tab.

The **General** tab options are explained as follows:

*   **Name**: This option provides a new name or modifies the current name of your farm
*   **Description**: This option provides a new description or modifies the current description of your farm

The **Security** tab options are explained as follows:

*   **Add**: This option aids to add new security groups that need to be farm administrators
*   **Remove**: This option aids to remove existing security groups that need not require to be farm administrators

The **Licensing** tab options are as follows:

*   **License server name**: This option provides the host name of your Citrix License Server Name
*   **License server port**: This option provides the port number that the license server should use; by default it is **27000**

In case you're planning to change the **Licensing** properties, it should be a planned maintenance activity, because a change in licensing servers requires the Provisioning Server stream service to be restarted on each Provisioning Server for licensing changes to take charge.

The following screenshot illustrates the **Licensing** tab:

- The **Options** tab options are as follows:
    - ° **Auto-Add**: If you're planning to use this option, tick the checkbox against the **Enable auto-add** feature, and then select the site that new target devices will be added to from the drop-down menu.

 This feature should be enabled when expecting to add new target devices. Leaving this feature enabled could end up with the system consuming vDisk space automatically even without any approval from the farm administrator.

    - ° **Auditing**: Enables or disables the auditing feature for this farm. By default it is disabled.
    - ° **Offline database support**: Enables or disables the offline database. This option helps the Provisioning Servers within the farm to use a snapshot of the database in the event of a database connection failure.

By default, it is disabled. Citrix recommends enabling it during production environment. Upon enabling the option, a snapshot of the database is formed and prepared at server startup. An offline database is continually updated by the stream process. If the database becomes offline, the stream process uses the snapshot to get information of the Provisioning Server and the target devices available to the target systems.

The following screenshot illustrates the **Options** feature:

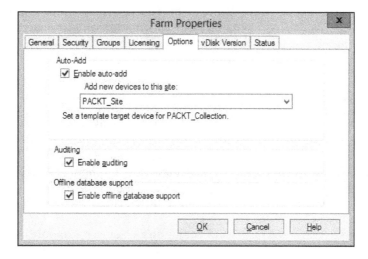

- The **vDisk Version** tab options are as follows:
  - ° **Alert if number of versions from base image exceeds**: This option aids to trigger an alert, in case number of versions from the base image is exceeded. The minimum value is **3** and the maximum value is **100**.
  - ° **Merge after automated vDisk update, if over alert threshold**: Enables the automatic merge feature should the number of vDisk versions exceed the alert threshold. Once checked, select the **Default access mode for new merge versions** option. Options include **Maintenance, Test (default)**, and **Production**. This is shown in the following screenshot:

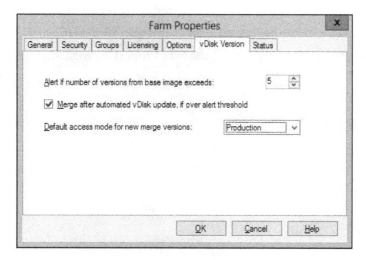

- The **Status** tab options are explained as follows:
  - ○ The current status of the farm offers database status information, if failover server, instance, and information on group access rights are being used

Operating sites

Operating sites on the Provisioning Server Console is a straightforward process, which helps to set up a site during installation as you have seen in *Chapter 2, Installing and Configuring Citrix® Provisioning Services 7.0*. A site is a collection of Provisioning Servers, vDisk pools, vDisk update management, device collection, views, and hosts. Creating a site is an operational function that can be performed with the following steps:

1. After connecting to a farm via **Provisioning Service Console**, right-click on the site and click on **Add new site**. The **Site Properties** wizard appears.

2. On the **General** tab, provide the name and a description for the site in the respective text boxes.

3. On the **Security** tab, click on the **Add** button to add security groups that will have the site administrator rights in your new site.

4. On the **Options** tab, in case new target devices are planned to be added using the **Auto-Add** feature, ensure you select the collection where target devices must be stored. This functionality can be added from farm properties as well.

To perform any modification in the existing site's properties, please perform the following steps:

1. Post connecting to a farm via **Provisioning Service Console**.

2. Right-click on the site in the Console and select **Properties**.

3. Make any changes required in the **Site Properties** wizard.

As you are now aware of how to create/modify the site, let us explore the site properties, using the **Site Properties** wizard. A new site can be added to a farm or any existing site can be modified as well. Each upcoming tab in the wizard allows us to configure a site. Site administrators can edit the properties of each site that they have access to. Now, let us explore each tab one by one.

- The **General** tab options are as follows:
  - ° **Name**: This option provides a new name or modifies the current name of your site in the textbox
  - ° **Description**: This option provides a new description or modifies the current description of your site in the textbox

- The **Security** tab options are explained as follows:
  - ° **Add...**: This option aids to add new security groups to administer at site level. For example, we have provided the **PACKTPVS\ Administrators** group.
  - ° **Remove**: This option aids to remove existing security groups that need not require to be site administrators. This is shown in the following screenshot:

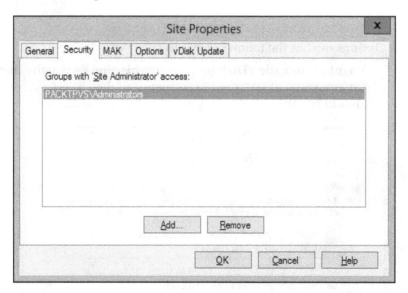

- The **MAK** tab authentication panel options are as follows:
  - ○ The **User** and **Password** options are for the MAK administrator user name and password. They must be provided, even before target devices use MAK on end points. This is shown in the following screenshot:

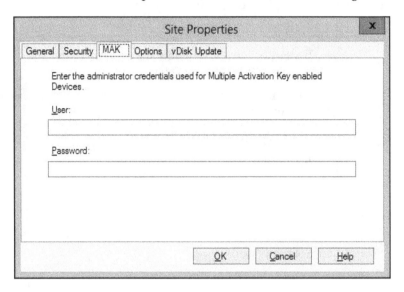

- The **Options** tab has the following features:
  - ○ **Enable automatic vDisk updates on this site**: Enable the checkbox for automatic vDisk occur to happen, and then select the server that should run the updates for your site.

- The **vDisk Update** tab feature is as follows:
  - ° **Enable automatic vDisk updates on this site**: Enable the checkbox and then select the server that should run the updates for your site. This is shown in the following screenshot:

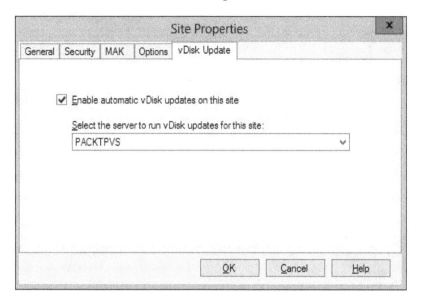

Managing and operating stores

A **store** is a logical name for a collection of vDisks arranged based on the way the vDisk folder is located. A farm contains one or more stores. The vDisk folder can exist in a Provisioning Server or on a shared storage, whenever we create a vDisk via Console, and it is directly assigned to a store.

From a permission standpoint, one or more Provisioning Servers within a site can access that store for the very purpose of providing a vDisk to target devices. The condition of providing vDisk to a target device is possible only if Provisioning Server results in successful identification of stores and locations where vDisk is available.

To increase the full flexibility of provisioning services within a farm configuration, it is always suggested to centralize the path of the vDisk storage locality. This is a condition to ensure high availability, in case one of the servers fails to provide the vDisk to the principal target device, the resiliency of another will provide the vDisk to it.

During the HA planning, please ensure that the storage path definition comes from a native MS clustering or from any third-party clustering. As a result, you will end up with availability of vDisk.

By default, a store can be created during the first run through of the provisioning service configuration wizard or it can be modified via the **Store Properties** wizard as well. Now, let us explore store properties. The **Store Properties** dialog includes the following tabs: **General**, **Paths**, and **Servers**.

- The **General** Tab options are explained as follows:
    - **Name**: This option provides a new name or modifies the current name of your site in the textbox.
    - **Description**: This option provides a new description or modifies the current description of your site in the textbox.
    - **Site that acts as the owner of this store**: This option is optional. View or scroll to choose the sites that will perform as the owner of the selected store. This is shown in the following screenshot:

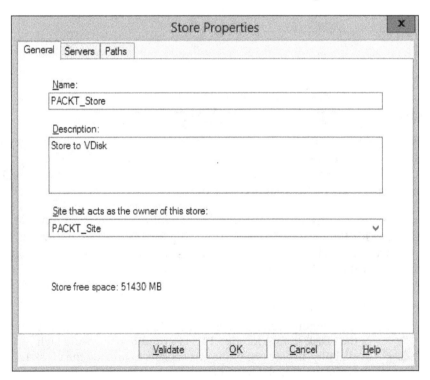

- The **Paths** tab options are explained as follows:

  ° **Default store path**: This option helps to view, provide, or browse for the physical path to the vDisk folder that the store represents. The default path is always used by all Provisioning Servers.

  ° **Default write cache paths**: This option helps to view, add, edit, remove, or move the default write cache paths for this store. Providing more than one write cache path allows for the vDisk load to be distributed physically to different drives. When a target device first connects and then stream service picks from the list. The order of the write cache paths, for any override paths in the server store properties, must match the order of the write cache paths specified here.

  ° **Validate**: This option helps to get validation results, which appear underneath the status column. This is shown in the following screenshot:

- The **Servers** tab options are explained as follows:

  ◦ **Site**: This option helps to view or scroll to select a site wherever Provisioning Servers can contact a store. Several sites can be contacted at the same store.

  ◦ **Servers that provide this store**: This option helps list Provisioning Servers within the selected site. Check the box next to all the servers that are permitted to access the store.

  ◦ **Validate**: This option helps to get validated results, which appear underneath the status column. This is shown in the following screenshot:

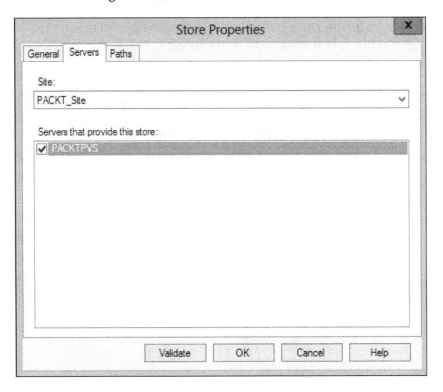

Managing and operating target devices

A **target device** is a virtual hard disk device that helps desktop/servers to boot and get applications from a vDisk over a network. A device that is castoff to create the vDisk image is defined as a principal (master) target device.

To set up a target device, we need to go through the following four stages:

- Stage 1: Readiness

    ◦ A principal (master) target device is essential to create a vDisk image

    ◦ A target device will use a vDisk image to boot up the system for the end user

- Stage 2: Inclusion of target devices to a collection in the farm

    ◦ Via Console

    ◦ Via auto-add

    ◦ Via import

    ◦ Allocating of target device

    ◦ Managing target devices within the farm

- Stage 3: Post creation of target device. The next step is to configure the device to boot over a network. In order to do so, we need to perform the upcoming steps:

    ◦ A vDisk should be allocated to the target device

    ◦ A bootstrap file should have been configured with necessary information for the device to boot from the assigned vDisk

- Stage 4: Booting target device over the network can be performed using the following two methods:

    ◦ Configuring the bootstrap file via Console

    ◦ Configuring the bootstrap file via manage boot devices utility

You have already seen both the methods in *Chapter 3, Managing Citrix® Provisioning Disk*, under the *Dealing with the bootstrap files and boot devices* section. Now let us understand target device properties.

The **General** tab options are explained as follows:

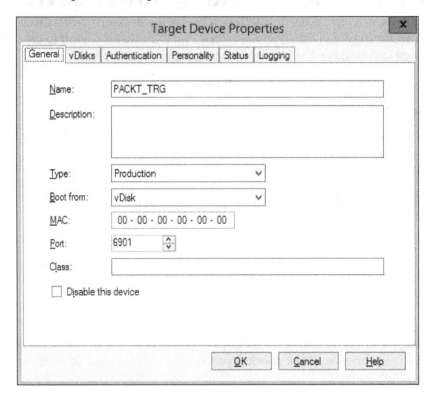

- **Name**: This option provides the name of the target device or the person's name who wants to use the target device. Please ensure that the target device name cannot be the same as the system name that is planned for provisioning.

- **Description**: This option provides a narrative associated with this target device.

- **Type**: This section provides options to aid access for the target device from the drop-down list. The options are as follows:
    - **Maintenance**: This option helps to place a device in the maintenance mode. A maintenance device has high-class read/write contacts to a maintenance edition; this is a stage before the test stage.

- ° **Test**: This option helps to place device in a test mode. Test devices have limited read-only access. To perform the test of a vDisk, identify the quality assurance in a standard image mode. This is a stage before the production stage.

- ° **Production**: This option helps the target device to stream an assigned vDisk into production for end user usage. A production device does not have any access to the maintenance edition or test edition. The device which is under the production stage has shared read-only access.

- **Boot from**: This option lets you select the boot method your target device should practice.

- **MAC**: This option provides the media access control address of the NIC, which is connected in the target system.

- **Port**: For this option, the default port number is **6901**, and it can be modified in case of any conflict.

- **Class**: This option provides the class used to match new vDisks to target devices.

- **Disable this device**: This option helps to prevent target devices from booting.

The **vDisks** tab options are as follows:

- **vDisks for this Device**: This option displays the list of vDisks allocated to this target device.

- **Add...**: This option aids to open the **Assign vDisks** wizard.

 Highpoint the vDisks to be allocated and click on OK.

- **Remove**: This option aids to remove vDisks from this device.

- **Printers...**: This option aids to open the **Target Devices vDisk Printers** wizard. This wizard allows you to choose the default printer.

Please refer to the following screenshot, to take a look at these options:

Authentication helps to boot the device. The **Authentication** tab options are listed as follows:

- **None**: No authentication is required.
- **Username** and **Password**: Username and password are already inbuilt. It cannot be modified. Changing the password is possible.
- External verification (third-party username and password for external verification).

Please refer to the following screenshot to review what we just learned:

The **Personality** section helps with secondary booting either from a local hard drive such as a boot device or with custom bootstraps possibilities. The **Personality** tab options are listed as follows:

- **Add...**: This option aids to parse the new bootstrap information
- **Edit...**: This option aids to modify the existing bootstrap information
- **Remove**: This option aids to remove the existing bootstrap information

Please refer to the following screenshot to take a look at these options:

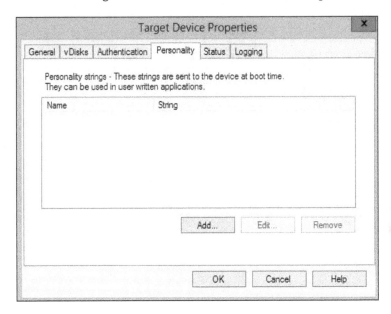

The **Status** tab option is listed as follows:

- **Current status of the device**: This option provides the status for each component, with required information such as Status, IP Address, Server, Retries, vDisk, vDisk version, vDisk full name, vDisk access, and License information. This is shown in the following screenshot:

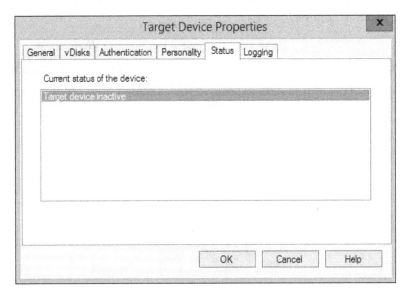

Logging can be configured with the following different options that aids towards monitoring status of disk. The **Logging** tab options are as follows:

- **Off**: Logging will be disabled
- **Fatal**: Records information that the system cannot recover due to failure.
- **Error**: Records information about system error at condition.
- **Warning**: Records information about system completes the action in case of open issues.
- **Info**: Records information against system's workflow.
- **Debug**: Records information against system log file.

Please refer to the following screenshot to take a look at these options:

Operation over target devices

Target devices are administered and scrutinized using the Citrix Provisioning Service Console along with Virtual Disk Status Tray utilities. In the Citrix Provisioning Service Console, actions that can be performed are listed as follows:

- Creating a new target device object in the Provisioning Service database
- Enabling the target device as the template for this collection
- Copying and pasting target device properties
- Booting of target devices
- Target device status checks via Console
- Sending messages to target devices
- Disabling target devices

Creating a new target device object in the Provisioning Service database

This operation can be performed with three different methods:

- Using the Provisioning Service Console to manually create a target device
- Using auto-add to create target device entries
- Using importing target device entries

To create a target device via the Citrix Provisioning Service console, please perform the following steps:

1. Open the Provisioning Service Console. Right-click on **Device Collection** and then select **Create Device**. As a result, the **Create Device** wizard pops up on screen.

2. Provide a name, description, and MAC address for the new target device in their respective textboxes.

3. In case a collection template is already available for this collection, you have to enable this option.

4. Click on the **Add device** button. The target device inherits all the properties from the template excluding the name of the target device and MAC address.

5. Click on **OK** to close the wizard. Now the target device is successfully created and allocated to a vDisk.

To create a target device via the auto-add feature, please perform the following steps:

1. Open **Provisioning Service Console**, right-click on the farm and then select the **Auto-Add** wizard. Now you should see a screen with a welcome message.

2. Click on **Next**. The **Enable Auto-Add** wizard appears. Enable the checkbox against the **Auto-Add** feature, and then click on **Next**. The **Select Site** page should be displayed now.

3. From the list, select the site in order to add the disk, and then click on **Next**. Select the default gathering or select a different gathering from the **Collection** list and click on **Next**, following which the **Select Template Devices** screen will be displayed.

4. Select the device to be used as a template, so that new devices being added will inherit the existing target device's basic property settings. Then click on **Next**.

5. Click on **Properties** in order to view the device's properties and then click on **Next**. The device name page gets displayed.

6. Provide a static prefix that helps identify all devices that are being added to the planned collection.

7. Provide the length of the incrementing number to subordinate with the devices being auxiliary to the planned collection.

8. Provide a static suffix that helps to identify all devices being added to this collection.

9. Click on **Next**. The final **Finish** dialog gets displayed.

10. Review all of your customized settings and then click on **Finish**.

As a next step, let us explore importing target devices into a collection. In order to do so, please perform the following steps:

1. On the Citrix Provisioning Service Console, right-click on the device collection that the target devices required to be imported and then click on **Target Device**. Go to **Import devices**. By now the **Import Target Devices** wizard will be displayed on screen.

2. Provide a location for a file to import. The target device information is read from the file and displayed.

3. Highpoint those target devices that need to be imported. In case you want to use a collection template for the imported target devices, enable the checkbox against the apply collection template device while creating devices.

4. You can import a .csv text file, containing target device information, into the selected collection by clicking on the **Import** option. At the end of the wizard, result will be displayed about the import status.

Setting the target device as the template for this collection

Target devices added to a target collection can be set as the template for a new target device. Properties from the template target device are inherited by a new target device.

To set a target device as the template device for a collection, please perform the following steps:

1. On the Citrix Provisioning Service Console, right-click on the target device.

2. Enable **Set device** as a template.

Copying and pasting target device properties

Personal vDisks that are used by target devices inherit the properties of the other devices. In order to perform copy and paste of target device properties, please perform the following steps:

1. On the Citrix Provisioning Service Console's details pane, right-click on the target device that you want to copy properties from, and then select **Copy Device Properties**. The **Copy Device Properties** wizard gets displayed.

2. Check against the properties that are required to be copied and then click on **Copy**. Now the properties are copied over to the clipboard and the wizard will disappear.

3. Right-click on target devices that want to take the same properties and then click on **Paste** from the menu option. The **Paste Device Properties** wizard gets displayed. Post copying completion, click on **Close**.

Booting target devices

In order to boot target devices, please perform the following operations:

1. On the Citrix Provisioning Service Console, right-click on a collection to either boot all target devices or select single target devices that you have planned to boot inside the collection.

2. Click on the **Boot devices** button to boot target devices. The **Status** column displays the **Boot Connect** status until the target device receives the communication, and then the status appears as **Success**.

Checking the target device's status via Console

To check the status of a target device, irrespective of whether it is active or inactive, please perform the following steps:

1. On the Citrix Provisioning Service Console, just double-click on the target device and then choose **Properties**. The device **Properties** tab appears.

2. Choose the **Status** tab and evaluate the following status information:
   - Current status — active (icon appears as green) or inactive (icon appears as black))
   - IP address
   - Present Provisioning Server
   - Present vDisk name
   - Provisioning Server cache file size in bytes

Sending messages to target devices

To send the message to a target device, whether it is active or inactive, please perform the following steps:

1. On the Citrix Provisioning Service Console, right-click on the collection to send a message to all members within the collection, or highpoint only for the selected target devices limited to the collection list that should receive the information, and then select the send message.

2. Provide a brief message to show on target devices in the **Message** textbox.

3. Click on the **Send Message** button. The **Status** column shows the message signal status once a target device successfully receives the information, and the status changes to **Success**.

Enabling/disabling a target device

To disable or enable a target device, please perform the following steps:

1. On the Citrix Provisioning Service Console, right-click on the target device.

2. Now select **Disable** or **Enable** from the pop-up list.

Managing and operating the device collections

A device collection offers the ability to create and administer logical security groups of target devices. Creating device collections simplifies device administration by carrying on actions at the collection level instead of the target device level.

Device collections are created and administered by farm administrators, site administrators who have security privileges to the site, or device administrators that have permission to the device collection.

- The **General** tab has the following options:
  - ° **Name**: This option allows you to provide a new name or modify the existing name of the device collection
  - ° **Description**: This option allows you to provide a new description or modify the existing description of the device collection

- The **Security** tab has the following options:
  - ° **Groups with Device Administrator access**: In this section, you can add or remove options to modify the security group under the device administrator

- ° **Groups with Device Operator access**: In this section, you can add or remove options to modify the security group under the device operator to perform operations such as booting and rebooting a target device, shutting down a target device, viewing the target device properties, and viewing vDisk properties for assigned target devices

- The **Auto-Add** tab has the following options:

    - ° **Template target device**: This option helps to select the target device from the drop-down list. You are also allowed to modify properties based on your privilege.

    - ° **Prefix**: By using this option, we can prefix auto-add, which will help to identify the security administrator.

    - ° **Length**: In this section, provide the length of the incrementing number to associate with the devices being added to this collection.

    - ° **Suffix**: By using this option, we can suffix auto-add, which will help to identify the security administrator.

    - ° **Last incremental number**: In this section, provide information about the last incremental number that was allocated to a device name in the target device collection.

You can have a look at all the options in the following screenshot:

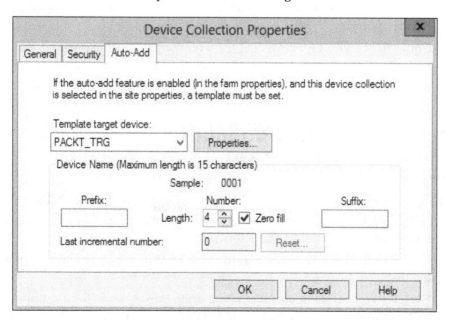

Device management operations

The list of operations that can be performed using the target device and associated functionality are listed as follows:

- Creating a device collection
- Importing target devices into collections
- Deleting collections and refreshing
- Boot target devices in a collection

Creating a device collection

Creating a device collection is a straightforward process and involves the following steps:

1. On the Citrix Provisioning Service Console, right-click on the device collections and select the **Create Device Collection** menu option. The **Device Collection Properties** wizard gets displayed.

2. On the **General** tab, enter a name of the device collection into the **Name** textbox and a description of the new collection device in the **Description** textbox.

3. Under the **Device Administrators** list, click on the **Add** button against **Security Group**.

4. Under the **Device Operators** list, click on the **Add** button against **Security Group**.

5. Click on **OK** to close.

Importing a device collection

To import target devices into a collection via Console, please perform the following steps:

1. On the Citrix Provisioning Service Console, right-click on the device collection that the target devices should be imported to. Click on **Target Device** and go to **Import Devices**.

2. The **Import Target Devices** wizard appears. Provide a location to import the file.

3. Highlight the target device that you plan to import, and click on **Import** to import the .csv text file that holds the device information into the selected collection. Click on **OK** to complete the wizard.

Deleting a device collection

To delete a target device collection, right-click on the collection folder that we want to delete on the Citrix Provisioning Service Console. Select Delete on the menu. A post deletion confirmation message gets displayed.

Booting target devices within a collection

To boot target devices within a collection, please perform the following steps:

1. On the Citrix Provisioning Service Console, right-click on the collection in the console tree and then navigate to **Target Device | Boot**. The **Target Device Control** dialog appears with the **Boot Devices** menu option selected in the **Settings** drop-down menu. Target devices appear in the **Device** table.

2. Click on the **Boot Devices** button to boot the target devices. The **Status** column shows the **Boot Signal** status until the target device successfully receives the signal and then changes to **Success**.

Managing views

The Citrix Provisioning Service Console's **Views** feature offers a method that permits us to quickly administer a group of devices. Views are normally created rendering to business requests, and farm administrators can form and administer views in the Console. The **View Properties** dialog allows you to view or make modifications to existing views. Now, let us explore **View Properties** tab by tab.

The **General** tab options are listed as follows:

- **Name**: This option allows you to provide a new name or modify the existing name of the view
- **Description**: This option allows you to provide a new description or modify the existing description of the view

You can have a look at these options in the following screenshot:

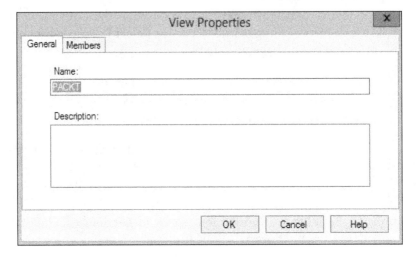

Members belonging to the view are listed under this tab with the option to add any new device or remove an existing device.

The **Members** tab options are listed as follows:

- **Add**: This option allows you to add new security groups to administer at view level. For example, we have provided the **PACKTPVS\Administrators** group.
- **Remove**: This option allows you to remove existing security groups, those security groups need not required to be a site administrator.

You can have a look at these options in the following screenshot:

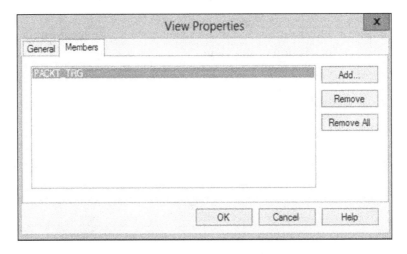

Managing and operating the provisioning servers

A **Provisioning Server** is a server that has provisioning stream services installed. They are utilized to stream vDisks on demand to target devices. Now let us explore the properties of Provisioning Servers.

The **General** tab options are listed as follows:

- **Name**: This option allows you to provide a new name or modify the existing name of the view.

- **Description**: This option allows you to provide a new description or modify the existing description of the view.

- **Power Rating**: This field displays the rating allocated to each server that is set for the purpose of identifying the least busy Provisioning Server. This action is performed by the farm administrator.

 By default, **Power Rating** is **1.0** and ranges between **0.1** and **1000.0**.

You can have a look at all the options in the following screenshot:

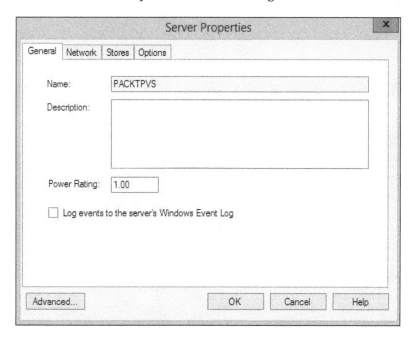

The **Network** tab options are listed as follows:

- The **Streaming IP Addresses** section options are listed as follows:
    - **Add...**: This option allows you to add the IP address of the chosen Provisioning Server
    - **Edit...**: This option allows you to modify the IP address of an existing Provisioning Server
    - **Remove**: This option allows you to remove an IP address of the chosen Provisioning Server

- The **Ports** section options are listed as follows:
    - By default **6910** is used. Port to designate a range of ports to be used by the stream service for target device communications.

You can have a look at all the options in the following screenshot:

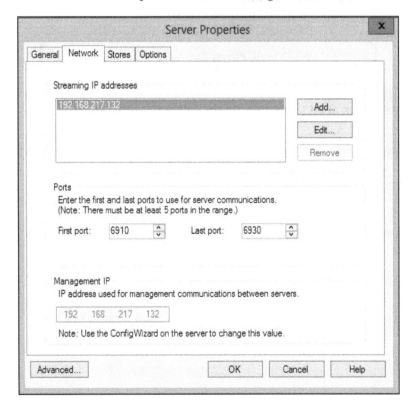

The **Stores** tab options are listed as follows:

- **Add...**: This option opens the **Store Properties** dialog to add stores; once this is changed, default settings are overridden
- **Edit...**: This option opens the **Store Properties** dialog to modify existing stores; once this is changed, default settings are overridden
- **Remove**: This option opens the **Store Properties** dialog to remove existing stores; once this is changed, default settings are overridden

You can have a look at all the options in the following screenshot:

The **Options** tab options are listed as follows:

- **Automate computer account password updates**: This option is used to modify the interval between renegotiations, when target devices are domain members and we need renegotiation of machine passwords between target devices and Windows AD
- **Enable automatic vDisk updates**: Check this option to enable vDisks to be updated automatically

You can have a look at these options in the following screenshot:

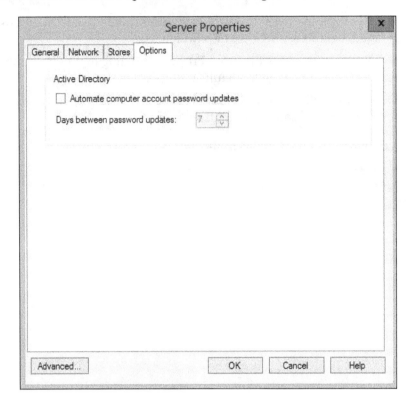

Operation tasks in the Provisioning Service task

The following is a list of the operational tasks that can be executed over the Provisioning Service administer part:

- Copying and pasting server properties
- Deleting a server
- Starting, stopping, or restarting Provisioning Services on a server
- Showing server connections
- Balancing target devices on a server
- Checking for vDisk access updates
- Configuring Provisioning Servers manually

Copying and pasting server properties

To copy the properties of one Provisioning Server to another Provisioning Server, please perform the following steps:

1. On the Citrix Provisioning Service Console, right-click on the Provisioning Server to copy properties from, and then select **Copy Server Properties**. The **Copy Server Properties** wizard gets displayed.

2. Check the checkbox against each property to copy. Now click on **Copy**.

3. On the Citrix Provisioning Service Console, right-click on the Provisioning Server that you want to copy the properties to and click on **Paste** from the menu option.

4. Once copying is completed, it will be displayed as successful.

Deleting a server

To delete the server from Provisioning Service Console, please perform the following steps:

1. On the Citrix Provisioning Service Console, highlight the Provisioning Server that you plan to delete and then select **Show Connected Devices** from the **Action** menu. Right-click on the menu, or on the **Action** pane. The **Connected Target Devices** dialog appears.

2. In the table of target devices, highlight all devices on the list and click on **Shutdown**. The **Target Device Control** dialog appears. Provide a message to notify target devices that the Provisioning Server is being shut down.

3. Scroll to select the number of seconds to delay after the message is received.

4. If the stream service is running on the Provisioning Server, stop the stream service.

5. Unassign all target devices from the Provisioning Server.

6. Highlight the Provisioning Server you want to delete, choose **Delete** from the **Action** menu, and then right-click on the menu, or on the **Action** pane. A delete confirmation message appears.

7. Click on **Yes** to confirm the deletion. The Provisioning Server is deleted and no longer shows in the Console.

Starting, stopping, or restarting Provisioning Services on a server

To perform operations such as starting, stopping, or restarting Provisioning Services on a Provisioning Server, please perform the following steps:

1. Choose the Provisioning Server in the Citrix Provisioning Service Console and then choose **Stream Services**. The **Provisioning Server Control** dialog appears.

2. Choose any one of the following operations that you want to perform:
   - **Start**: This option aids to start Provisioning Services
   - **Stop**: This option aids to stop Provisioning Services
   - **Restart**: This option aids to restart Provisioning Services, in case any changes have been made on the Provisioning Server

3. Post start/stop/restart, a confirmation will be displayed on the screen. Click on **Close**.

Showing the server connections

To perform operations such as viewing and administering all target device connections to the Provisioning Server, please perform the following steps:

1. Choose the Provisioning Server in the Citrix Provisioning Service Console. Select **Display the connected devices** and the **Connected Target Devices** wizard gets displayed.

2. Select one or more target devices in the table to perform any of the following connection tasks:
   - **Shutdown**: This option aids to shut down target devices that are planned for maintenance
   - **Reboot**: This option aids to reboot target devices that are planned for maintenance
   - **Message**: This option aids to send massage to all target devices that are planned for maintenance

Load balancing the target devices on a server

You will want to enable load balancing for target devices for the purpose of high availability. To do so, please perform the following steps:

1. On the Citrix Provisioning Service Console, and then right-click on the vDisk in the Console and choose **Load Balancing**. The **vDisk Load Balancing** wizard gets displayed.

2. Now enable load balancing based on the subnet affinity or rebalance enabled using trigger percent.

Checking for vDisk access updates

Checking vDisk update status can be accomplished with the following steps:

1. Right-click on the Provisioning Server in the **Details** pane and choose the **Check for updates** option.

2. Click on **Automatic Update** and then click on **OK** on the confirmation message that appears.

Manually configuring Provisioning Servers

Configuring Provisioning Servers manually is an easy process. First, check whether Provisioning Service is up and running. It is isn't, please perform the following steps to start the BOOTP Service, TFTP Service, or PXE Service:

1. Log in to a Windows machine, go to the Start menu, and click on **Run**.

2. Next, type `service.msc` in the box provided.

3. Now you will see a new **Services** window. Right-click on the service you want to start and click on **Start**.

Operating vDisks

vDisks are nothing but virtual hard disks for a target system; such disks are generally available in Provisioning Server or in storage clusters. The vDisk file type is VHD; its associated properties files will end up with the extension `.pvp` and a chain of differencing disks with the extension `.avhd`.

Creating vDisks

Our next step is to explore the process of creating a vDisk image file. During the creation of a vDisk, the basic considerations are as follows:

- Check that there is enough storage space either on the Provisioning Server or in shared storage.

- Ensure disks are formatted either using FAT or NTFS for Windows OS to recognize.

- NTFS-based disk allows maximum of 2 TB of disk and FAT-based disk allows maximum of 4096 MB.

- vDisks can be created in two formats. One is standard image mode, which can be shared across multiple machines, and the other is private image mode, which can be used by only one target device.

- The readiness of the master target device for imaging; you are already aware about the process of preparing the target device explained in *Chapter 3, Managing Citrix® Provisioning Disk*.

Now, let us learn about creating a vDisk. In order to create a vDisk, please perform the following steps:

1. In the Citrix Provisioning Service Console, right-click on **vDisk Pool** under the **Site** section, where you have planned to place the vDisk, and then choose **Create vDisk**. The **Create vDisk** wizard gets displayed.

2. If you have accessed this wizard from **vDisk Pool** under the **Site** section, choose the store where your vDisk should reside from the drop-down menu. If you have accessed this wizard from the store, choose the site where this vDisk should be added from the drop-down menu choose the Provisioning Server that will create the vDisk.

3. Provide a file name in the **Name** box and provide a brief description in the **Description** box for your new vDisk. In the **Size** textbox, provide an appropriate size for the new vDisk file.

4. The next step is to provide a VHD format. Set the format as either **Fixed** or **Dynamic**. If you have planned for the dynamic size of emulating, SCSI should be 2040 GB and 127 GB for VHD emulating IDE.

5. Click on **Create vDisk**. Once the vDisk is successfully created, it is displayed in the Citrix Provisioning Service Console's **Details** pane and is ready to be formatted.

6. Right-click on the vDisk in the Citrix Provisioning Service Console and choose **Mount vDisk**.

This is the overall process involved in the creation of a vDisk. Now, let us go ahead and explore creating common images for use with Citrix XenServer VMs and physical devices or blade servers, one by one, in the upcoming section.

Creating vDisk images

Let us get started with configuring a common image for Citrix XenServer VMs and physical servers to consume.

Prerequisites for building common images for XenServer, we need to have:

- Citrix XenServer Platinum Licensing
- The ability of the local network to support over PXE, and DHCP

To create a common image that boots from a physical or virtual machine, the first step is to prepare the master target device — the server you have planned as principal (master) target device. As always, first ensure that a supported Windows operating system is installed along with the appropriate latest patches. Then, install Provisioning Services on the principal (master) target device. In order to do so, please perform the following steps:

1. Log on to the principal (master) target device as a domain administrator or a domain user with full access to the machine.
2. Now, map the Provisioning Server target device software on the physical machine and start the installation with the default settings.
3. Post installation, reboot the system and complete the installation.

Post successful installation, our next step is to install the Xenconvert on the principal (master) target device. The Xenconvert standalone utility can be downloaded at www.xenserver.org or from the Citrix download page.

Installation of Xenconvert is a straightforward process, and after successfully installing Xenconvert on the target device, convert the physical machine into virtual machine and send it to Xenserver., and followed by that install Xenserver Tools on the VM.

Next, use either the **Provisioning Services Imaging** wizard or Xenserver to create a virtual disk. After creation, the vDisk can be assigned to VMs in the standard mode.

Now let us explore creating a common image for blade servers. In order to create a common image using the common hard drive method that boots from heterogeneous blade servers, we need to perform the following steps:

1. Use the Citrix Provisioning Service Console to create a new vDisk file.

2. Log on to the blade server and create a new system:

    1. Install the OS.

    2. Install System Pack (installs all drivers).

    3. Install all required OS updates.

    4. Install the Provisioning Services target device software on the system.

3. Enable PXE boot from the new system's hard disk drive, and then verify that the system can access the vDisk.

4. Prioritize the vDisk in new systems as a bootable hard disk drive.

5. Install the operating system and reboot the systems, and then verify that NIC drivers are installed.

6. Perform the imaging. Once it is complete, assign the vDisk in the standard mode, allocate it to two different systems, and boot it up.

Summary

In this chapter, we learned about managing and operating farms, sites, stores, target devices, target device collections, and Provisioning Servers. We also covered managing views and operating vDisks.

In the upcoming chapter, we will learn about upgrading Citrix Provisioning Service and vDisk.

5
Upgrading Citrix® Provisioning Farm and vDisk

With the knowledge gained in *Chapter 4, Operating Citrix® Provisioning Services 7.0*, you will have understood the operating farm, store, site, target device, target device collection, Provisioning Server, view, and creating a vDisk. In this chapter, we will learn about requirements, mandatory actions to perform farm and vDisk upgradation.

In this chapter, we will cover the following topics:

- Upgrading the existing Provisioning Services farm
- Upgrading vDisks
- Troubleshooting references articles

Upgrading the existing Provisioning Services farm

Citrix supports Provisioning Services farm upgrades for the version starting from 5.1 SP1, 5.1 SP2, 5.6, 5.6 SP1, 6.x, and so on. To upgrade the existing Provisioning Services farm, please follow the given steps:

1. Three mandates that need to be followed before each and every upgrade are:
   - Back up the existing Provisioning Services database
   - Place the Provisioning Services Server in the maintenance mode
   - Back up all vDisks associated with the farm

2. After following the preceding mandates, the next step is to get into execution of the upgrade. In order to do so, first we have to upgrade the first Provisioning Server. As a result it should also upgrade the Provisioning Services database. The first Provisioning Services upgrade is done as follows:

    1. Uninstall the existing Provisioning Services software.

    2. Reinstall the Provisioning Services software. The configuration of Provisioning Services can be performed as you have read in *Chapter 2, Installing and Configuring Citrix® Provisioning Services 7.0.*

 The database is upgraded when the first Provisioning Server is upgraded. This is a parallel activity.

Citrix recommends closing all the opened up Provisioning Services Consoles till the upgrade is finished. This really helps in order to overcome any errors or any failure in upgrade operations.

3. Post the successful upgrade of the first Citrix Provisioning Server and database, the next step is to upgrade the remaining Provisioning Servers inside the farm and upgrade the Citrix Provisioning Service Console.

    Repeat the preceding procedure that was performed on the first Provisioning Server on every other Provisioning Server in the farm. This will result in the successful farm upgrade. vDisk can be upgraded with two methods based on the consumption, either the Hyper-V method or Reverse Imaging method.

The Hyper-V method

The following procedure illustrates the method of upgrading vDisks using the Hyper-V method as the tool to install new versions of the Provisioning Service drivers and the rest of the target device modules. This method significantly shortens the upgrade process and reduces the sum of tasks that need to be done. Please follow these steps to use the Hyper-V method:

1. On your planned Hyper-V host, in case the Provisioning Services are installed, please go ahead and uninstall it.

2. Install the latest version of Provisioning Services Server software, as you have learned in *Chapter 2, Installing and Configuring Citrix® Provisioning Services 7.0*, under installation of Provisioning Services.

3. Either copy the newly created disk or copy the existing VHD file to your planned Hyper-V host.

4. Using the Hyper-V Manager console create a new VM. Use the copied over vDisk on command prompt.

5. Post creation of VM on the Hyper-V Manger console, remove the NIC and add the legacy NIC, power on the VM, and the system will start installing the new driver required. Post installation the system will reboot.

6. Post reboot VM will have the power on. Now go ahead and uninstall the existing Provisioning Services target device software (if any) and reboot the system.

Installing Hyper-V Integration Services (optional)

Installing Hyper-V Integration Services is essential while VHD is bootable. In order to install Integration Services, please mount the Integration Services disk and perform the following steps:

1. Start to install the Provisioning Services target device software as you have learned in *Chapter 3, Managing Citrix® Provisioning Disk*.

2. Once the Provisioning Services target device is installed, select the option to bind Provisioning Services to the inactive NIC.

3. Power of the virtual machine, under **Properties**, prioritizes the legacy NIC to boot first.

4. Move VHD (vDisk.vhd) to the Provisioning Server.

5. Now let us go ahead and add the VHD to the Provisioning Services DB.

6. Add the Hyper-V VM to the group of target devices and associate the vDisk with respect to accurate target devices.

7. Quickly verify if vDisk is set to Standard Image mode. If not, please set to Standard Image mode.

8. Along with that please ensure that vDisk is set to PXE first. If not, please set it to PXE boot on BIOS and power on the VM.

Upon the successful completion of the preceding procedure, the original vDisk is now upgraded and a common image between the physical and virtual machine has been created and communication established between them.

The Reverse Imaging method

Now let us move on to using the Reverse Imaging technique including three procedures that are vDisk upgrade version, automated upgrade, and manual upgrade. Let us get started with the vDisk upgrade version. To use the vDisk upgrade method, please perform the following steps:

1. Go ahead and boot the maintenance device from the managed vDisk when it is under the planned maintenance mode.

2. From the Provisioning Services installed directory, run `P2PVS.exe` to converse an image using volume-to-volume imaging. Choose the vDisk as the source and the hard disk drive as the foundation. If your destination partition is on a partition, we have to edit the `boot.ini` or `bcedit` partition settings before rebooting the system(HDD).

3. Now, let us go ahead and reboot the maintenance device from the system's HDD.

4. On the maintenance device, we have to uninstall a 6.x target device and then the newer version.

5. Now go ahead and run the Provisioning Services Imaging wizard to create a new vDisk image, as always, create the target device (incase it does not already exist), and then allocate the vDisk to your planned target device.

6. Test the streaming of your newly created vDisk image by booting the maintenance device or else perform the test of the device from the upgraded vDisk.

Automated upgrade helps to reduce the manual effort involved in the preceding process. In order to do so in your production, please follow the upcoming steps:

1. Over the master target device, that is under the maintenance device, depending on the target device OS architecture, run either `PVS_UpgradeWizard.exe` or `PVS_UpgradeWizard_x64.exe`.

2. Copy over `upgradeManager61.exe` from the Provisioning Services 6.1 target device installed directory, into the installation directory of the Provisioning Server.

3. On your planned Provisioning Server, run `UpgradeManager61.exe`.

4. On your planned master target device, run `UpgradeConfig.exe` from the product installation folder. In order to execute the EXE file, please perform the following steps:

    1. Provide a local account with administrator privileges to `AutoLogon`. This local account cannot have an empty password.

2. Provide a local partition to which the Reverse Imaging method will clone the data. The original hard drive that the vDisk was cloned from is recommended.

 If this is a new hard drive, please use the manual upgrade method to initialize the hard drive.

3. Provide the Provisioning Server IP address, and a user account and password to connect to the upgrade manager. This account cannot have an unfilled password. Click on **OK**.
4. Upgrade config performs a sanity check on various parameters. If everything passes, the upgrade config exits, and then reboots the machine to start the upgrade script.
5. The system will reboot a number of times and then display a message to indicate that the script execution has been successfully completed.

Manual upgrade is a straight forward process. It can be considered only when the following conditions conditions apply:

- Over Private Image mode, vDisk may have gone through a number of modifications
- In case the hard drive is no longer available on the system

Updating vDisks

Updating an existing vDisk is required in many cases in a production environment as well as in a non-production environment. The process of updating vDisk will be created with a new version and end with no modifications on the base image vDisk. Updating vDisk is a three-step process, which is as follows:

- The first step is to create a vDisk either via the manual method of creating or autocreation or through merge mechanism.
- The second step is to boot the freshly created vDisk from the target system.
- The third step is to promote the newly created vDisk version with a stage-by-stage approach such as maintenance, test, and production.

Manual vDisk creation

In order to create a new version of vDisk manually, please perform the following steps:

1. On the Citrix Provisioning Services Console, right-click either on a vDisk inside a device collection or on a vDisk pool, and then choose the version. The vDisk versions wizard is shown.

 Verify that the vDisk is currently not in Private Image mode.

2. Now click on **New**. The new version shown in the wizard, with access set to the maintenance mode and manual update method, is set.

3. Under the maintenance mode, boot the vDisk and then install or remove applications or add the required patches. Perform the test in order to check whether the changes made are in line with your plan. If so, shut down the device that is under the maintenance mode.

 While booting a test or maintenance device, the boot menu displays options that allows the user to select a vDisk or version of that vDisk to boot from.

4. Right-click on the vDisk and promote to maintenance.

5. Perform the required testing and move from the test stage to the production stage. Click on **OK** to promote this particular version to end user usage and complete the successful maintenance.

Automatic vDisk creation

Automatic creation of vDisk is recommended for Standard Image mode usage only. Private Image mode can be performed using any standard software distribution tool.

 Switching the vDisk from Private Image mode to Standard Image mode is not the right method; the disk may end up with serious issues.

The requirement for performing vDisk updates automatically requires the following activity to happen:

- Enabling automatic vDisk updates and assigning the dedicated Provisioning Server within the site to perform updates across all servers within its reachability

The procedure to create a vDisk automatically is as follows:

1. On the Citrix Provisioning Console, right-click on the site. The site properties wizard is displayed.

2. On the **vDisk Update** tab, enable the check against **Enable the automatic vDisk updates**.

3. Scroll to select the server to run vDisk updates for this site, and then click on **OK**.

The next step is to configure the virtual pool for automatic updates to occur. In order to do so, please perform the following steps:

1. On the Citrix Provisioning Console, under the vDisk update management node, right-click on **Hosts**, and then choose the **Add Host** tab. The **Virtual Host Connection** wizard is displayed.

2. Click on **Next** to begin. The hypervisor page appears.

3. Select the radio button against the listed hypervisor (either Citrix XenServer, VMware vSphere/Microsoft Hyper-V/SCVMM) used by this pool, and then click on **Next**.

4. Provide the name and description against the virtual host connection and click on **Next**.

5. Provide the virtualization hostname or the IP address, username, and password to register, and click on **OK**.

The next step is to create a VM and configure ESD (supported ESD are WSUS and SCCM), which will be used to update the vDisk across.

Virtual machines which are planned to update a managed vDisk should be created on supported hypervisors such as Citrix XenServer, Microsoft Hyper-V, and VMware vSphere, and prior to configuring vDisk Update Management.

Managing update tasks

vDisk Update Management utilizes VM to process updates to managed vDisk(s). vDisks are created in the Citrix Provisioning Service Console. Post creation of the vDisk, add it to the vDisk update manager, as managed vDisks, via the **Managed vDisk Setup** wizard. In order to do so, please perform the following steps:

1. On the vDisk Update Management node, in the Citrix Provisioning Services Console, right-click on vDisks and choose the **Add vDisks** option. The **Managed vDisk Setup** welcome screen is displayed. Click on **Next** to begin. The vDisk screen should be displayed.

2. Choose the default search options for all the stores and servers, and further choose one or more vDisks to be managed. Then click on **Next**. The host/VM screen should be displayed.

3. Choose the type of connection to use when hosting the VM from the appropriate drop-down list.

4. Provide the name of the update VM used to course the vDisk update and click on **Next**. The AD administrator tool will be displayed.

5. On your active directory, provide a domain name and **Organizational Unit (OU)** to create an AD system account that will be cast off by the update device that is created exclusively for updating this vDisk, and then click on **Next**. The confirmation screen should be displayed.

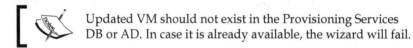

Updated VM should not exist in the Provisioning Services DB or AD. In case it is already available, the wizard will fail.

6. Evaluate all configurations and then click on **Finish**.

The update VM will boot, install updates, and reboot as necessary. Once the update task is successfully completed, VM will be shut down.

The update status can be checked from the Citrix Provisioning Service Console tree under vDisk Update Management. Following this, go to vDisks (vDisk name) to see the completed update status. The status can also be checked using the event viewer or in WSUS.

Merging of the vDisk from the existing disk

vDisk can be merged from the update disk either by creating a new base image or by using a consolidated differencing disk. It helps to save disk space and increase scalability and performance, based on the merging method opted. Let us go ahead and explore about merging to a new base image.

The process of merging chains of differencing disks and base image disks, via creating a new base image or full merge on the merging of disks, is the next version in the chain. Whenever a merge is planned, a new disk image should be created. The biggest advantage of using this method is the increase in performance other than the disk space:

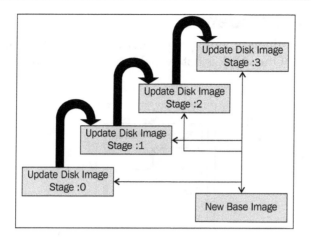

The process of merging a partial chain of differencing disks is up to the final version. The advantage of using this increased disk space is that it is quicker than performing a full merge. This method is highly recommended when storage or remote network bandwidth is limited. Now, let us go ahead and understand the real operational steps behind merging differencing disks. Please perform the following steps for the same:

1. On the Citrix Provisioning Service Console, right-click on vDisk, and then select the version from the **Menu** option. Now the vDisk version wizard is displayed.

2. Click on **Merge**. The merge wizard is displayed. Choose either the **Full merge** or **Partial merge** option:

    1. **Full merge** can be opted for if you need to merge along with the base image.

    2. **Partial merge** can be opted for if you need to merge excluding the base image with reference to the original base image.

3. After selecting the method of merge, the next step is to select the access mode from the list (production, test, and maintenance). Post selection, click on **OK** to begin with the process of merging.

4. After a successful merging, the new version is shown in the vDisk version's wizard.

Promoting the update version

The process of promoting is not bringing a device directly to the production stage; an updated version of the vDisk is not available to target systems until it is moved to production.

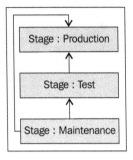

The update promotion disk is a three-stage process, starting from **Maintenance** followed by **Test**, with the final stage being **Production**, as illustrated in the preceding screenshot.

Each time a new version is created, by default the access setting configuration is automatically set to the maintenance mode to allow maintenance devices to make operations including read/write updates. Post completion of updating, this particular version can be promoted from maintenance to test, to perform operations with the read-only option to allow for testing by the test target system, or directly from the maintenance stage to the production stage.

Troubleshooting reference articles

We have now completed all operations that a Citrix administrator and Citrix engineer should know for the Citrix Provisioning Services product management. The following table refers to some of the known issues and solutions available in the Citrix support site at `http://support.citrix.com/article/`. Please refer to them in case any of the listed issues occur:

Article ID	Possible issue description
CTX128276	Configuring KMS licensing for Windows and Office 2010 and 2013.
CTX139405	Target devices PXE boot error: Max number of DHCP retries exceeded.
CTX132995	Provisioning Services Console error is displayed during KMS activation.
CTX139498	Provisioning Services target devices boot slow in ESX 5.1.
CTX139478	Write cache set to the Provisioning Services target device falls back to the server.

Article ID	Possible issue description
CTX131484	Target device login request timed out.
CTX133065	Best practice for setting the Citrix Profile Manager cache file for the Provisioning Server.
CTX139265	How to enable HTML5 connections to Provisioning Services-based catalogues.
CTX129105	How to use **Multiple Activation Key (MAK)** activation with automatic updates.
CTX117874	XenServer and Provisioning Server port usage information.
CTX128301	How to reverse image from a virtual disk to a local hard disk with VMware ESX4.
CTX127815	Desktops do not register using XenDesktop and Provisioning Server.
CTX125086	How to capture a memory dump from a provisioned target in the VMware environment.
CTX118263	Error: STOP: 0x0000007B. After updating the virtual machine tools.
CTX117374	Best practices to configure Provisioning Server on a network.
CTX130744	Errors: "Insufficient system resources exist to complete the requested service" and "The system has reached the maximum size allowed for the system part of the registry. Additional storage requests will be ignored."
CTX133272	Error: vDisk is not available. Please check your network PXE boot configuration and restart the imaging wizard.

Summary

In this chapter, you have learned about requirements, mandate actions to upgrade Citrix Provisioning Services, upgrading vDisk, and a list of reference articles that helps in basic troubleshooting for administrators/engineers. Thanks once again for choosing this book.

Index

Thank you for buying
Getting Started with Citrix®
Provisioning Services 7.0

About Packt Publishing

Packt, pronounced 'packed', published its first book "Mastering phpMyAdmin for Effective MySQL Management" in April 2004 and subsequently continued to specialize in publishing highly focused books on specific technologies and solutions.

Our books and publications share the experiences of your fellow IT professionals in adapting and customizing today's systems, applications, and frameworks. Our solution based books give you the knowledge and power to customize the software and technologies you're using to get the job done. Packt books are more specific and less general than the IT books you have seen in the past. Our unique business model allows us to bring you more focused information, giving you more of what you need to know, and less of what you don't.

Packt is a modern, yet unique publishing company, which focuses on producing quality, cutting-edge books for communities of developers, administrators, and newbies alike. For more information, please visit our website: www.packtpub.com.

About Packt Enterprise

In 2010, Packt launched two new brands, Packt Enterprise and Packt Open Source, in order to continue its focus on specialization. This book is part of the Packt Enterprise brand, home to books published on enterprise software – software created by major vendors, including (but not limited to) IBM, Microsoft and Oracle, often for use in other corporations. Its titles will offer information relevant to a range of users of this software, including administrators, developers, architects, and end users.

Writing for Packt

We welcome all inquiries from people who are interested in authoring. Book proposals should be sent to author@packtpub.com. If your book idea is still at an early stage and you would like to discuss it first before writing a formal book proposal, contact us; one of our commissioning editors will get in touch with you.

We're not just looking for published authors; if you have strong technical skills but no writing experience, our experienced editors can help you develop a writing career, or simply get some additional reward for your expertise.

Getting Started with Citrix XenApp 6.5

ISBN: 978-1-84968-666-2   Paperback: 478 pages

Design and implement Citrix farms based on XenApp 6.5

1. Use Citrix management tools to publish applications and resources on client devices with this book and eBook

2. Deploy and optimize XenApp 6.5 on Citrix XenServer, VMware ESX, and Microsoft Hyper-V virtual machines and physical servers

3. Understand new features included in XenApp 6.5 including a brand new chapter on advanced XenApp deployment covering topics such as unattended install of XenApp 6.5, using dynamic data center provisioning, and more

Implementing Citrix XenServer Quickstarter

ISBN: 978-1-84968-982-3   Paperback: 134 pages

A practical guide to getting started with the Citrix XenServer Virtualization technology with easy-to-follow instructions

1. A simple and quick start guide for any system admin who wants to step into the latest and hottest virtualization technology

2. Learn how to convert physical machines to virtual ones using XenConvert

3. Get to grips with the advanced features of Citrix XenServer

Please check **www.PacktPub.com** for information on our titles

Getting Started with Citrix® CloudPortal™

ISBN: 978-1-78217-682-4   Paperback: 128 pages

Get acquainted with Citrix Systems® CPSM and CPBM in order to administer cloud services smoothly and comprehensively

1. Overview of CPSM and CPBM architectures, and planning CPSM and CPBM

2. Become efficient in product management, workflow management, and billing and pricing management

3. Provision services efficiently to cloud consumers and clients

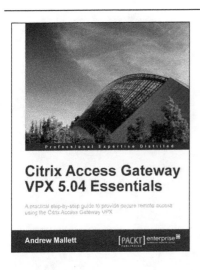

Citrix Access Gateway VPX 5.04 Essentials

ISBN: 978-1-84968-822-2   Paperback: 234 pages

A practical step-by-step guide to provide secure remote access using the Citrix Access Gateway VPX

1. A complete administration companion guiding you through the complexity of providing secure remote access using the Citrix Access Gateway 5 virtual appliance

2. Establish secure access using ICA-Proxy to your Citrix XenApp and XenDesktop hosted environments

3. Use SmartAccess technology to evaluate end users' devices before they connect to your protected network

Please check **www.PacktPub.com** for information on our titles